LIFE AND LIBERTY AN AMERICAN HISTORY

Volume 2: 1789 to 1877

AUTHORS

Philip Roden teaches American history at Evanston Township High School in Evanston, Illinois. Over the past 20 years, he has also taught in Nigeria, John Marshall High School on Chicago's West Side, and Northwestern University in Social Studies education. He is the author of *The Elusive Truth* and co-author of *Promise of America*, both textbooks published by Scott, Foresman.

Robynn L. Greer has taught for 12 years at North Clayton Senior High School in Clayton County, Georgia. She has been a classroom teacher and department chairman during those years, as well as being active in the Georgia Association of Student Councils. She has a master's degree in social studies and is pursuing a specialist degree. Greer has won numerous awards for classroom teaching, including the Star Teacher award and Outstanding Young Educator.

Bruce Kraig is Associate Professor of History and Continuing Education at Roosevelt University in Chicago, Illinois, where he teaches courses in American history and Contemporary America. He has also conducted archaeological excavations of American colonial sites. Besides writing numerous professional articles in his field, Dr. Kraig writes a regular newspaper column and does a radio program devoted to popular science and archaeology. He is a co-author of *Eastern Hemisphere*, part of the Scott, Foresman Elementary Social Studies series.

Betty M. Bivins, Social Studies and Reading Advisor for 14 secondary schools in the Los Angeles Unified School District, is responsible for teacher training and curriculum development. Earlier, as teacher and reading coordinator at Taft High School in Woodland Hills, California, she developed a school-wide reading program. A classroom teacher for 26 years, she is also the author of professional articles, course outlines, and curriculum materials for teachers.

Teacher Consultants
The following consultants, all of whom teach or have taught American history at the high school level, read and critiqued this book during its development. They provided valuable comments on the context, organization, and level of difficulty to make *Life and Liberty* a practical classroom text.

Mary Louise Dunn
Teacher
Hope High School
Providence, Rhode Island

Sybil Etters
Social Studies Department Chairperson
Independence High School
Charlotte, North Carolina

Tony Navarro
Teacher
Pasadena High School
Pasadena, California

Ruth Pearcy
Teacher
Gainesville High School
Gainesville, Texas

Joyce Stevos
Social Studies Area Supervisor
Providence School Department
Providence, Rhode Island

Dr. Betty L. Waugh
Social Studies Department Chairperson
West Mesa High School
Albuquerque, New Mexico

ISBN 0-673-13462-8

Copyright © 1984
Scott, Foresman and Company, Glenview, Illinois
All Rights Reserved. Printed in the United States of America.

This publication is protected by Copyright and permission should be obtained from the publisher prior to any prohibited reproduction, storage in a retrieval system, transmission in any form or by any means, electronic, mechanical, photocopying, recording, or otherwise. For information regarding permission, write to:

Scott, Foresman and Company, 1900 East Lake Avenue, Glenview, Illinois 60025

12345678910-VHJ-9291908988878685848 3
Acknowledgments for illustrations and quoted matter are included on page 151. This page is an extension of the copyright page.

LIFE AND LIBERTY

AN AMERICAN HISTORY
Volume 2: 1789 to 1877

Philip Roden   Robynn L. Greer

Bruce Kraig   Betty M. Bivins

SCOTT, FORESMAN AND COMPANY
EDITORIAL OFFICES: GLENVIEW, ILLINOIS

REGIONAL OFFICES:
Palo Alto, California   Oakland, New Jersey
Tucker, Georgia   Dallas, Texas
Glenview, Illinois

CONTENTS

Maps

Biographies

Pioneers hold a party to beat flax for weaving.

A YOUNG NATION

1789–1815

America in the period from 1789 to 1815 might be compared to a class of students in their last year of school. Those students are at a crossroads in their life, almost independent but not quite. Many have an idea of where they are going but aren't exactly sure how they are going to get there.

Between 1789 and 1815 the United States was not really sure where it was going. The country was at a crossroads.

The Constitution was the blueprint for building the government, and so the people did have one outline. But having an outline and filling it out are two different things. This job was left to political leaders. Some of them left lasting marks on the nation's government and history.

For the average person in this period, the future held many promises. Opportunity and success waited if the person worked hard, took a few chances, and had some luck. The lands west of the Appalachians waited. Thousands moved westward hoping for a new beginning, a better life, or a chance to make more money.

In these years, Americans began to take pride in being Americans. Americans were proud that the area of the country doubled and the population almost tripled during this period. These feelings were one reason the United States fought another war with England. That war is sometimes called America's second war for independence.

In this unit, you will learn how the United States government was put together. You will get a taste of how it was to move west, and you will see what types of people went west. You will also see how feelings of national pride changed Americans.

TIME LINE

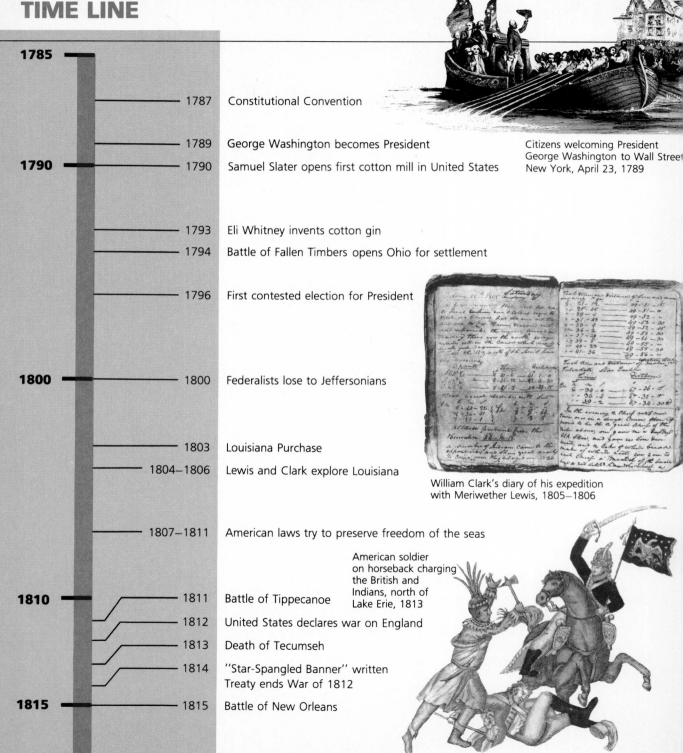

1785	
1787	Constitutional Convention
1789	George Washington becomes President
1790	
1790	Samuel Slater opens first cotton mill in United States
1793	Eli Whitney invents cotton gin
1794	Battle of Fallen Timbers opens Ohio for settlement
1796	First contested election for President
1800	
1800	Federalists lose to Jeffersonians
1803	Louisiana Purchase
1804–1806	Lewis and Clark explore Louisiana
1807–1811	American laws try to preserve freedom of the seas
1810	
1811	Battle of Tippecanoe
1812	United States declares war on England
1813	Death of Tecumseh
1814	"Star-Spangled Banner" written Treaty ends War of 1812
1815	
1815	Battle of New Orleans

Citizens welcoming President
George Washington to Wall Street
New York, April 23, 1789

William Clark's diary of his expedition
with Meriwether Lewis, 1805–1806

American soldier
on horseback charging
the British and
Indians, north of
Lake Erie, 1813

CHAPTER 12

Politics, 1789–1815

Between 1789 and 1815, Americans began to view one person—the President—as the nation's leader. Before this period, the United States had not had a political leader who represented the country as a whole.

In Section 1 of this chapter, you will study about the first President, George Washington. In Section 2, you will read how political parties formed. In Section 3, you will study how Thomas Jefferson ran the government. In Section 4, you will study the War of 1812.

SECTION 1 The First President

In February, 1789, the electoral college met and **unanimously** (without exception) elected George Washington President. Washington, a Federalist, supported the Constitution and wanted a strong central government. The votes for him showed that he was really the only choice for President and that many Americans backed the Constitution.

Problems of the New Nation
When he took office on April 30, 1789, Washington faced four major problems. First, he had to find ways to unite Americans. Many opposed the government. Washington knew people must believe in the government for it to succeed.

Second, he needed to persuade other countries to respect the United States. The English remained in some of their forts on American land and refused to leave. Also, several countries refused to trade with the United States.

Third, he had to find ways to pay the country's debts. The government had an empty treasury, yet it had not paid back everyone who loaned money to fight the Revolutionary War. The United States owed about $50 million to foreign countries and to the American people. The state governments owed about $25 million.

Fourth, the nation had little gold or silver money. People used paper money that changed in value depending upon how much money was printed. The country needed a stable currency.

Glossary terms

unanimous
excise tax
neutral
tradition

3

MERCY OTIS WARREN
(1728–1814)

One person who saw firsthand how America's new leaders served was Mercy Otis Warren of Massachusetts. The sister of one Revolutionary leader (James Otis) and the wife of another (James Warren), she knew most of the leaders of the American Revolution and the United States government well.

Before the Revolution began, she wrote several plays that poked fun at English leaders and helped win support for the American side. After Americans won independence, she began writing poetry and history.

Her most famous work was *A History of the Rise, Progress, and Termination of the American Revolution.* Because she knew so many leaders and was present at many important events, she included information that no other historian could.

As a woman, she could play no part in making political decisions for the country, but she could report how politics was changing its leaders. A strong supporter of Jefferson, she criticized leaders who thought they were better than the rest of the American people.

Museum of Fine Arts, Boston

Congress set up four executive departments to help solve these problems: State, to deal with other countries; Treasury, to work on the nation's money problems; War, to defend the United States; and Justice, to enforce laws of Congress. The heads of these departments became Washington's main advisers, or Cabinet. His most important advisers were Secretary of State Thomas Jefferson and Secretary of the Treasury Alexander Hamilton.

Hamilton's Financial Plan

To solve the country's money problems, Alexander Hamilton believed he had to meet four goals:
- pay the debts owed by the United States
- pay the war debts owed by the states
- create a source of income for the United States
- organize a sound money and banking system

To meet these goals, Hamilton got Congress to pass laws saying the United States government would pay, in full, its own debts and the states' war debts. He said that paying off loans in full would show that America kept its word.

Hamilton then needed $75 million to pay what the nation owed. Hamilton had two ideas to raise the money.

First, he proposed a high tariff, or tax on imports. He said that if the tariff made imported goods cost more than goods made in the United States, Americans would buy American goods. He wanted to use the tariff to promote American business as well as to raise money.

Second, he asked Congress to pass an **excise tax**. An excise tax is one on goods made or sold within a country. This tax angered many people, but it appeared likely to raise money.

To provide a sound money supply, Hamilton proposed setting up a national bank. He wanted it to handle government loans and debts and to hold money collected as taxes. Jefferson opposed the bank, saying it would give too much power to rich people and be unfair to state and local banks. He also said a national bank was unconstitutional, because the Constitution said nothing about such a bank. However, Washington took Hamilton's side, and Congress agreed to set up the Bank of the United States.

Results of Hamilton's Program

Hamilton's plans met with mixed successes and failures. The United States gained respect from other countries by trying to pay what it owed, and the national bank provided a sound money supply. But the financial program was not perfect. The excise tax, on whiskey in particular, led to a test of the government's strength.

Because of poor transportation, farmers in western Pennsylvania could not easily take their corn to eastern markets. For that reason, they turned their corn into whiskey and then sent it to market. Twenty-four bushels of corn made two kegs of whiskey. Whiskey was many farmers' only cash "crop," and the excise tax on it greatly cut their income. Many farmers rebelled by refusing to pay the tax, and some attacked the tax collectors.

Hamilton urged Washington to use soldiers to end the rebellion and show the government's strength. Washington and Hamilton led 13,000 troops against the rebels in 1794.

Hamilton had proved his point. Americans could see that the young government was strong. But his action angered many farmers and led to a clash with Jefferson.

Foreign Affairs

While Washington was in office he faced problems with France, Spain, and England. He signed treaties with England and Spain that increased American trade. Treaties also led those countries to pull most troops out of the land between the Appalachian Mountains and the Mississippi River.

Reading Skills

Some words act as links between ideas. Look up the words listed to see some ways that such words operate.
1. Fourth (page 3, last paragraph) points to:
   a. fourth event
   b. fourth problem
   c. fourth solution
2. However (page 4, next to last paragraph) shows:
   a. contrast   b. time   c. more

George Washington and Alexander Hamilton lead troops against the whiskey rebels.

5

Washington's biggest problem in foreign affairs concerned France. Soon after the French Revolution began in 1789, the French asked the United States for help. Many Americans wanted the United States to give France the same kind of help the French had given Americans during the Revolutionary War. Other Americans, mostly Federalists, disagreed. They said that helping the French would pull the United States into France's war with England. They said the United States was not strong enough for a major war.

Washington finally issued a statement in 1793. He told both the French and the English that the United States would be **neutral.** It would not take sides in any foreign war. Washington's decision was not popular, but it did keep the country out of war.

Washington's Accomplishments

Washington retired in 1797 after serving eight years in office. He refused to serve a third term, and this action began a **tradition.** Not until 1940 did any President serve more than two terms.

By the time Washington retired he had helped establish a strong central government and a strong financial system. He also had won respect for America both from foreign countries and from Americans themselves.

SECTION 1 REVIEW

1. What four major problems did George Washington face when he became President?

2. How did Hamilton plan to raise the money needed to pay the nation's debts?

3. What was the cause of the Whiskey Rebellion? How did Washington and Hamilton end the rebellion? What did their success prove?

Glossary terms

political party
platform
nominate

SECTION 2 Political Parties Form

Have you ever had to work with someone whose beliefs were different from yours? Even though you disliked this person's ideas, did you have to support the person's position and help him or her out? If so, you were in a position like that of two of America's greatest leaders, Alexander Hamilton and Thomas Jefferson. As members of Washington's Cabinet, they had to work together, but they argued over

Hamilton's money and banking plans and about foreign policy. Because of their conflicts, Jefferson resigned from Washington's Cabinet in 1793.

The underlying problem between Hamilton and Jefferson lay in their beliefs about how government should be run. Their ideas led to the founding of two **political parties.** Study the following chart to learn about their beliefs.

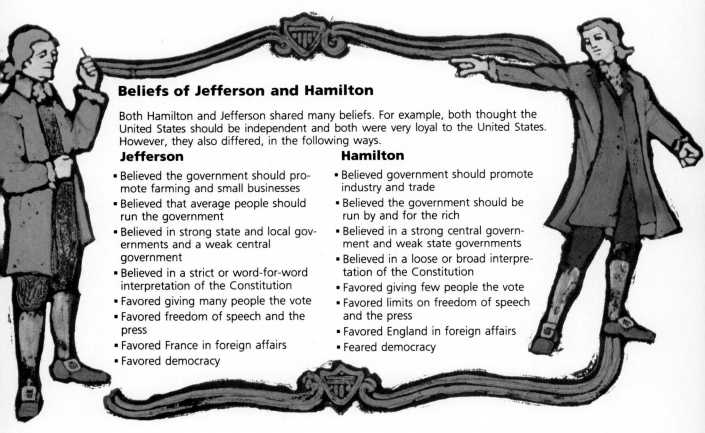

Beliefs of Jefferson and Hamilton

Both Hamilton and Jefferson shared many beliefs. For example, both thought the United States should be independent and both were very loyal to the United States. However, they also differed, in the following ways.

Jefferson

- Believed the government should promote farming and small businesses
- Believed that average people should run the government
- Believed in strong state and local governments and a weak central government
- Believed in a strict or word-for-word interpretation of the Constitution
- Favored giving many people the vote
- Favored freedom of speech and the press
- Favored France in foreign affairs
- Favored democracy

Hamilton

- Believed government should promote industry and trade
- Believed the government should be run by and for the rich
- Believed in a strong central government and weak state governments
- Believed in a loose or broad interpretation of the Constitution
- Favored giving few people the vote
- Favored limits on freedom of speech and the press
- Favored England in foreign affairs
- Feared democracy

Questions

1. Which man favored a loose interpretation of the Constitution? Which man favored a strict interpretation?
2. Which man mainly supported farmers? Which man mainly supported manufacturers and merchants?
3. Which man was afraid of the common people? Which man thought government should be open to them?

Reading Skills

Study the chart above to determine the following:
1. The left column represents:
   a. Jefferson's views
   b. Hamilton's views
2. The two men disagreed upon:
   a. 3 ideas   b. 4 ideas   c. 8 ideas

CANDIDATES: 1796

ELECTORAL VOTE BY STATE

FEDERALIST
John Adams 71 ■

REPUBLICAN
Thomas Jefferson 68 ■

139

CANDIDATES: 1800

ELECTORAL VOTE BY STATE

REPUBLICAN
Thomas Jefferson 73 ■

FEDERALIST
John Adams 65 ■

138

The numbers show how many electoral votes each of the states cast for President. For each state, this number equals the number of representatives and senators in Congress. The colors tell which party won these votes.

The Rise of Political Parties

Both men attracted followers. Voters and candidates for office began forming political parties based on the ideas of the two men. People who backed Hamilton's ideas called themselves Federalists. Followers of Jefferson called themselves Republicans.

What parties do. Americans formed parties because a political party can do the following:

1. provide a **platform** that candidates agree to follow. A platform is a statement of a party's beliefs and a list of the plans it will follow if its members win office.

2. **nominate** candidates for office. In the election of 1796, party members in Congress chose their party's candidates for President. Today, conventions or voters do this job.

3. organize support for candidates. Parties urge people to vote, hold rallies, and help pay for running for office.

Early party elections. In the elections of 1792 and 1794, a few candidates for Congress ran for office as Federalists or Republicans. By 1796, political differences were far more open. When Washington refused to run for a third term, both parties chose candidates for President. At that time, candidates for President and Vice-President did not run as a pair. In the 1796 election, John Adams, a Federalist, received the most votes and became President. Thomas Jefferson, a Republican, came in second and became Vice-President.

Changes in parties. The two parties that formed around the ideas of Hamilton and Jefferson did not stay the same. Jefferson's party won such wide support that the Federalist party gradually disappeared. However, the Republicans also changed. In the 1820s, they formed two groups—Democratic-Republicans and National Republicans. The Democratic-Republicans shortened their names and became the Democratic party. The National Republicans took up many Federalist ideas and called themselves Whigs. When their party died out, yet another new party formed, the modern Republican party. The two main parties today, the Democrats and the Republicans, trace their roots to Hamilton and Jefferson.

SECTION 2 REVIEW

1. Name two problems that Hamilton and Jefferson clashed over.
2. Describe the three jobs political parties can do.
3. According to the maps, which parts of the country favored Adams in 1796 and 1800? Which parts favored Jefferson? Which parts switched sides in 1800?

SECTION 3 Jefferson as President

inauguration

When John Adams became President in 1797, it was one of the earliest examples in world history of a large country's leader peacefully taking over from another leader. However, Adams, like Washington, was a Federalist. He continued the Federalist programs Washington had begun. A more important change came after the election of 1800, when Thomas Jefferson and his followers won control of the presidency and of Congress. Many Federalists feared that Jefferson's party would destroy all they had done.

Jeffersonian Changes

Jefferson did not destroy the country as the Federalists predicted, nor did he change all that they had done. In his first speech as President, he made it clear that he wanted to unify Americans by stating: "every difference of opinion is not a difference of principle. . . . We are all Republicans; we are all Federalists."

Jefferson was the first President to take the oath of office in the new capital city, Washington, D.C. He started his term by changing a few traditions. While both Washington and Adams rode to their **inauguration** ceremonies in coaches drawn by white horses, Jefferson walked. He also refused to wear a powdered wig and changed many of the formal practices that Washington had started.

Jefferson did not fire all the Federalists who held government jobs. However, he did appoint Republicans to any openings.

President Jefferson changed some Federalist programs. He asked Congress to repeal the unpopular tax on whiskey. He also had Congress cut the wait for immigrants to become citizens from 14 years in the country to 5 years.

Congress also repealed the Judiciary Act of 1801. This law had allowed President Adams to appoint many new judges—all Federalists. The Federalists had passed the law after they lost the election of 1800 but before they left office. They had hoped that by passing this law they could control at least one branch of government—the courts.

But Jefferson did not end all the Federalist programs. He kept the United States Bank in business and continued the plan to pay the government's debts. In fact, he even used a loose interpretation of the Constitution to buy more land.

Election day in Philadelphia

Pierre Toussaint L'Ouverture

Reading Skills

Decide if each statement about Jefferson below is (a) <u>stated</u>, or (b) an <u>inference</u> (a conclusion based on what is stated):
1. He changed traditions.
2. He was a good leader.
3. He thought before he acted.
4. He bought the Louisiana Territory.

Glossary terms

underlying cause
immediate cause
spark
blockade
impress
nationalism

The Louisiana Purchase

One of the most important things Jefferson did as President was to double the size of the United States. He did this by buying the Louisiana Territory (much of the land between the Mississippi River and the Rocky Mountains) from France in 1803. (See map on page 22.)

Jefferson had heard that Spain had secretly traded the Louisiana Territory to France. This worried Jefferson because the important port of New Orleans was in Louisiana. Jefferson decided to try to buy the port from France. However, before American diplomats had a chance to make an offer to Napoleon Bonaparte, the ruler of France, Napoleon approached them. He offered to sell the United States not just New Orleans but all of the Louisiana Territory—for $15 million.

Jefferson did not think he had power to buy this land. He wanted permission from Congress, but he did not have time to get it. After searching his soul, Jefferson decided to accept Napoleon's offer.

Napoleon wanted to sell this rich territory for two reasons. First, slaves in France's island colony of Haiti in the Caribbean had overthrown the French government there. In 1791, led by Pierre [pē'ar] Toussaint L'Ouverture [tü san' lü ver tyr'], the slaves had won their independence. Without Haiti, Louisiana was of little use to Napoleon. Second, Napoleon needed money—fast. He was about to begin several costly wars that he hoped would make him ruler of Europe. Jefferson gained from Napoleon's problems.

SECTION 3 REVIEW
1. What changes did Jefferson make in the government?
2. How did Jefferson acquire the Louisiana Territory?
3. Why was Napoleon willing to part with Louisiana?

SECTION 4 The War of 1812

Napoleon's wars caused problems that led the United States to fight England in the War of 1812. That war is often called the second war for American independence.

Causes

"One thing leads to another" is a way of saying that one act may lead to important results. However, a result can have more than one cause and more than one kind of cause.

For example, Mark Ikler came home from school one day, took off his shoes, and turned on the TV set. When his mother came home, she was upset because her car had stalled on a busy road. She was carrying a bag when she entered the living room, and so she didn't see Mark's shoes. She tripped over the shoes and began yelling:

"Can't you ever pick up after yourself? I've told you a thousand times not to leave your shoes in the middle of the floor."

Her yelling had at least three causes:

1. **The underlying cause.** This cause was a situation that had existed for a long time: Mark often left his shoes or clothes wherever he took them off.

2. **The immediate cause.** This cause had existed for a short time: Mark's mother was angry because her car stalled.

3. **The spark.** This cause was the incident that made her lose her temper: She tripped over Mark's shoes.

Trying to figure out what caused events in history isn't as simple as trying to find the causes of anger, but events also have underlying causes, immediate causes, and at least one spark. Read about the War of 1812 and try to decide what caused it.

Background of the War

Throughout Jefferson's first term as President, the United States traded with both England and France. Although those two countries went to war in 1803, not until Jefferson began his second term in 1805 did their war hurt the United States. At that time, England announced that it would not allow freedom of the seas. England set up a **blockade** of French ports in both Europe and the Caribbean Sea to stop neutral countries from selling goods to France. The English captured American ships that tried to trade in these ports. The French also did not allow freedom of the seas and tried to stop the United States from trading with England.

The issue of freedom of the seas involved more than just trade. It also involved sailors. The English stopped American ships and searched them for sailors who had deserted England's navy. That navy was well known for poor food, low pay, and cruel captains. If the English found sailors on American ships who spoke with an English accent or did not have proper papers, they **impressed** them—forced them to serve in the English navy. In some cases, they impressed Americans into the English navy. This angered Americans.

Tecumseh [tə kum′sə] was a Shawnee chief who dreamed of uniting all the Indians east of the Mississippi into one large group or confederation. He wanted all tribes to pledge that they would sign no more treaties to give up their lands.

With his brother Tenskwatawa [tən skwä tä′wä] the Prophet, in 1805, he began trying to persuade members of other tribes to join his group. This was hard because each tribe had different customs and laws.

In 1811, while Tecumseh was in the South trying to gain support of other tribes, American troops led by Governor William Henry Harrison marched near his village at Tippecanoe Creek in the Indiana Territory. Fearing an attack, Tenskwatawa led the Indians to attack Harrison's troops. American soldiers defeated the Indians at the Battle of Tippecanoe. When Tecumseh returned home, he found the Indians scattered and his dream shattered.

Still hoping to defend Indian lands, Tecumseh joined the English army in the War of 1812. As a general, he persuaded other Indians to join the English side.

Tecumseh was killed in 1813 at the Battle of the Thames in Ontario, Canada. With his death came the end of the Indian confederation and the end of his dream.

For five years, beginning in 1807, President Jefferson and, after him, President James Madison (elected in 1808) tried to use laws to promote freedom of the seas. At the request of Jefferson and Madison, Congress passed laws about trade. One law cut off trade with all countries. A later law cut off trade only with England and France.

In 1811, hoping to end English and French interference with American trade, President Madison tried yet another law. He said that the United States would (1) trade with the first of the two countries that agreed to respect American trading rights, and (2) refuse to trade with the other country. Napoleon said he would respect American rights. Madison therefore said that the United States would trade with France but not with England.

By this time, the results of the 1810 election were being felt. In 1810, many members of Congress lost to young men from the West and South. These young men were called the "War Hawks."

Like the voters they represented, the War Hawks wanted to go to war. One reason was land hunger. Western farmers looked for new land to settle and found Canada inviting, but Canada was an English colony. Southerners wanted to move into Florida, which was then owned by Spain, England's ally.

Growing feelings of national pride, or **nationalism,** were yet another reason. Many Americans were tired of being pushed around by the English. They itched for a good fight that would settle once and for all that Americans were independent of England.

Another reason was the desire to end Indian raids. Many farmers believed that the English in Canada and the Spanish in Florida encouraged Indians to raid American settlements by promising the Indians that they could get their land back.

In November, 1811, American troops led by Governor William Henry Harrison battled Indians at a village on Tippecanoe Creek in the Indiana Territory. In the village, the Americans claimed to find weapons made in England. They pointed to these weapons as proof that England was behind Indian raids.

The leaders of the War Hawks in Congress demanded that the United States go to war with England. They said that the only way to end Indian raids, as well as gain freedom of the seas, was to attack England's land in Canada and Spain's land in Florida.

Unfortunately, neither the telephone or telegraph had yet been invented. Had there been either in 1812, war might have been avoided. Letters took weeks to get from the United States to England. When English leaders heard in June, 1812, that Americans were preparing for war, they lifted their blockade of American ships. Five days later, the United States declared war. For several weeks neither country knew what the other had done.

Question

Make a chart with these headings: "Underlying Causes," "Immediate Causes," and "Spark(s)." Then list each of these causes of the War of 1812 under the heading you think correct: impressment of American sailors, interference with trade, land hunger, desire to end Indian raids, election of War Hawks, nationalism, Battle of Tippecanoe, slow mails between England and the United States. Be ready to explain why you listed the causes as you did.

A Nation at War

The United States was not ready for war in two important ways: (1) Both the army and navy were small and poorly

The American ship *Constitution* fights the English ship *Guerriere* in August, 1812. Nicknamed "Old Ironsides," the *Constitution* now is docked in Boston Harbor.

equipped. (2) Many Americans, especially those in New England, opposed the war. Although James Madison won reelection as President in November, 1812, New Englanders did not support him. Those who depended upon trade for a living thought that "Mr. Madison's War" would ruin them. They tried to pass laws limiting the government's power.

Luckily for the United States, the English were busy fighting the French. Until the English defeated the French in Europe in 1814, the battles in America were small. Some were victories for the English, some for the United States.

Peace talks had begun when the war started. By 1814, since both sides were tired of fighting a war that was going nowhere, they decided to stop fighting. On Christmas Eve, 1814, they signed the Treaty of Ghent, which ended the war.

However, just as slow mails kept people from knowing the war had started, slow mails kept them from knowing it had ended. Two weeks after the war ended, General Andrew Jackson led an army of white and black frontiersmen and pirates against the English at the Battle of New Orleans. For Americans, the fighting ended in victory.

Results

In the war, neither side gained land nor settled anything about freedom of the seas or impressment. But both the United States and England gained better relations. From this point on, they settled their differences through treaties, such as those setting the 3,000-mile-long boundary between the United States and Canada.

The War of 1812 also marked a turning point for business. Before the war, the United States looked to England and France for industry and trade. The lack of trade from 1807 on encouraged American industry. By war's end, the United States was more self-reliant.

After this war, America turned its face from Europe and looked west for its future. The United States did not get deeply involved in events in Europe for another 100 years.

SECTION 4 REVIEW

1. Describe three reasons Americans declared war.
2. Which section of the country most opposed the war? Which sections most strongly supported the war? Why?
3. How did Tecumseh and Tenskwatawa hope to keep settlers out of Indian lands?
4. What did the United States gain from the war?

Reading Skills

Read the last five paragraphs on this page to decide the following: Which pieces of information listed below are clearly stated? Which are inferences—ideas not stated directly, but suggested by what is said?
1. The United States gained no territory in the war.
2. The war brought friendly relations between England and the United States.
3. The war encouraged American industry.
4. The War of 1812 was not a major war.
5. The War of 1812 revealed how slow the mails were.

CHAPTER 12 ACTIVITIES

Wordpower!

Crossword puzzle:

```
¹U ²N D E R L Y I ³N G C A U S E
   O               E
   M               U
   ⁴I M M E D I A T E C A U ⁵S E
   N               R         P
   A               A         A
   T             ⁶P L A T F O R M
   E                         K
```

Make up clues for each term in the crossword puzzle.

Across	Down
1.	2.
4.	3.
6.	5.

Reading Skills

Choose the best title for each list below.

List 1

- freedom of the seas
- national pride
- War Hawks
- land hunger

Titles

a. Problems the United States Faced
b. Reasons for the War of 1812
c. Difficulties Between the United States and England

List 2

- better relations with England
- greater economic independence
- less interest in European affairs

Titles

a. Results of the War of 1812
b. Reasons the United States Went to War
c. Good Effects of the War of 1812

Writing Skills

This chapter describes the important work of Washington, Hamilton, and Jefferson. For each man, make a list of three or four of his major accomplishments. Be sure to write each entry in the list in a complete sentence.

Figure It Out

Francis Scott Key wrote the following poem after watching the English attack Fort McHenry in Maryland during the War of 1812. Set to music, the poem became our National Anthem in 1933. Read Key's words below. Then answer the questions.

> O say, can you see, by the dawn's early light,
> What so proudly we hailed at the twilight's last gleaming,
> Whose broad stripes and bright stars, through the perilous fight,
> O'er the ramparts we watched were so gallantly streaming?
> And the rockets' red glare, the bombs bursting in air,
> Gave proof through the night that our flag was still there.
> O say, does the star-spangled banner yet wave
> O'er the land of the free and the home of the brave?

1. Where was the flag flying that Key saw?
2. Did the rockets and bombs help him see the flag or block it from his view? Explain how you know.
3. At what time of day did Key see the flag?
4. In your own words, write out the two questions that Key asked in his song.
5. The "Star-Spangled Banner" became the National Anthem because it described something of which the nation could be proud. What was that something?

CHAPTER 13

Glossary term

social mobility

Society and Business

Although more than 200 years have passed since the United States became independent, 1776 is not so long ago. There are Americans living today who when they were young looked into the eyes of Americans born in the early 1800s, and some of those people looked into the eyes of people who took part in the Revolution. Americans today are linked to 1776 by just three long lifetimes. However, in each of those three lifetimes, people have faced great changes in society, business, and government.

This chapter looks at changes early in United States history. Section 1 describes society after the Revolution. Section 2 is about changes in business between 1787 and 1815.

This detail from the painting *The Picnic*, done by an unknown artist about 1800, shows one way friends got together at this time.

SECTION 1 Social Mobility

American society is often described as a ladder. Each social class is a different rung on the ladder, and people can move from one social class to another just as they can move up or down a ladder. Moving from class to class in this way is called **social mobility.**

Climbing the Social Ladder

Most Americans believe that anyone who works hard can move into a higher social class. This idea was turned into fact in the late 1700s and early 1800s as more and more people began to move up the social ladder. American social classes after the Revolutionary War were especially open to change for five main reasons.

First, Americans passed laws against titles of nobility. In other countries, such as England and France, only people born with noble titles made up the upper class.

Second, in the United States, large plots of land in the West sat waiting for someone to buy or farm them. In other countries, class often depended upon how much land a family owned, but it was almost impossible for most people to save enough money to buy land.

Third, new laws changed how families passed wealth on. In England, only the oldest son inherited land and wealth. In

America, a family's land could be divided among all the children in the family.

Fourth, many of the Loyalists who left America during the Revolution were from the upper classes. They left openings at the top of the social ladder. Middle-class people took their place as community leaders.

Fifth, many immigrants arrived from other countries, usually taking the lowest jobs in society. They pushed people who came before them up the social ladder.

A Modern Example

Today, social mobility is likely to come through education and work as well as by owning land. Consider the story of Larry Cobb.

Larry was born in Georgia in 1956 into a family of tenant farmers. When he was five, the family moved to Atlanta and lived in a small apartment in a tough part of town. As the oldest of six children, he learned responsibility early.

When Cobb was in the sixth grade, the family returned to the farm, and he worked in the fields picking heavy crops. He decided right then that this work was boring, backbreaking, and not for him.

In high school, Cobb found that the strong muscles he developed doing farm work helped him in sports. He made the football team and became a leader in the Student Council. After winning a scholarship to the University of Pennsylvania, he joined the track team as a hammer-thrower. As team captain, he traveled to Europe and many parts of the United States.

After graduation, he worked for a large insurance company, but he dreamed of becoming a lawyer. He entered law school in 1981, his goals and education having helped him move up the social ladder.

Figuring the Score

In any competition, be it war or baseball, someone wins and someone loses. Study the scoreboard on the next page to see how the Revolution changed life in the United States. Then decide whether the average American won or lost.

On your paper, number from 1 to 20 and make two columns. Label one column *plus* (+) and the other *minus* (−). For each item on the scoreboard, put a plus next to its number if you think average people gained and a minus if you think they did not.

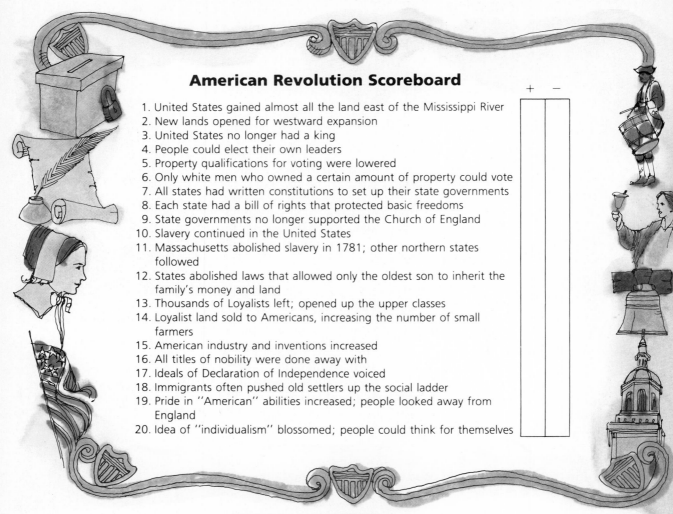

American Revolution Scoreboard

		+	−

1. United States gained almost all the land east of the Mississippi River
2. New lands opened for westward expansion
3. United States no longer had a king
4. People could elect their own leaders
5. Property qualifications for voting were lowered
6. Only white men who owned a certain amount of property could vote
7. All states had written constitutions to set up their state governments
8. Each state had a bill of rights that protected basic freedoms
9. State governments no longer supported the Church of England
10. Slavery continued in the United States
11. Massachusetts abolished slavery in 1781; other northern states followed
12. States abolished laws that allowed only the oldest son to inherit the family's money and land
13. Thousands of Loyalists left; opened up the upper classes
14. Loyalist land sold to Americans, increasing the number of small farmers
15. American industry and inventions increased
16. All titles of nobility were done away with
17. Ideals of Declaration of Independence voiced
18. Immigrants often pushed old settlers up the social ladder
19. Pride in "American" abilities increased; people looked away from England
20. Idea of "individualism" blossomed; people could think for themselves

SECTION 1 REVIEW

1. How many pluses (+) did you have? How many minuses (−)? Did the American people win or lose in the Revolution? Explain.
2. Which three items on the scoreboard do you think most influenced the American people? Why?
3. What changes would you have made on the scoreboard in the year 1790 if you could have? Why?
4. Give five reasons for greater social mobility after the Revolution.
5. Do you think social mobility is still possible in America? Why or why not?

SECTION 2 American Business

As the 1700s gave way to the 1800s, businesses were growing and changing. Inventions led to new industries and to changes in farming. Many Americans, ready to take advantage of any opportunity, found that they faced new chances to do well.

Methods of Work

Important changes arose in ways of working. The first settlers in America had made most of their own clothes, shoes, candles, and other goods by hand. About 1740, craft workers began taking over these jobs, making goods to order for those who could afford them. Many craft workers settled in the cities and towns of the Northeast. They worked alone or with a few others at home or in small shops.

In the late 1700s, inventors in England made some new machines that changed how things were made there. One new machine was the spinning jenny. It could spin cotton into thread much faster than a spinning wheel. Another was the power loom, which rapidly wove thread into cloth. Water power operated both machines. Spinning and weaving factories, called mills, were built near waterfalls. The falling water turned water wheels that ran the machines.

Glossary term

cotton gin

Samuel Slater (above) built the first cotton mill in the United States (below).

A small word that can add to or interfere with your understanding of what you read is the word it. Read the first paragraph on this page carefully to decide the following:

1. In the phrase "made it illegal," it refers to:
   a. export of machines
   b. export of plans
   c. mechanics to leave the country
2. In the sentence beginning "It wanted to keep the secrets of these machines . . . ," it refers to:
   a. Parliament
   b. England
   c. cotton or wool

These machines allowed England to make and sell much more cloth than any other country. For that reason, Parliament passed laws against the export of machines or their plans and made it illegal for mechanics to leave the country. It wanted to keep the secrets of these machines in England.

Two Inventors

The work of two men during the late 1700s was particularly important in helping America's own infant industries to grow. One man was Samuel Slater, who came to the United States from England in 1789. Slater had been attracted by the news that several state governments would pay a bonus to anyone who could build cloth-making machines. Slater's answer to England's laws was to memorize the working of the latest cotton-spinning machines and to pass himself off as a farmer.

After arriving in America, Slater became a partner with two other men and set up the first cotton mill in the United States. Located at Pawtucket, Rhode Island, the mill was a big success.

Slater's mill would not have had enough cotton to spin if not for the work of a young American, Eli Whitney. After finishing college in 1792, Whitney had gone south to teach. At dinner one night, friends told him that a fortune could be made growing cotton if only a way could be found to remove the sticky seeds from the cotton fiber. A slave could remove the seeds by hand from only 1 pound of cotton a day.

Whitney spent the next ten days inventing a machine, called the **cotton gin,** to remove seeds from cotton. By April, 1793, he had made a gin that could clean 50 pounds of cotton in a day.

Word of Whitney's machine spread like fire in the South. People came to see his work, and many copied his machine. Study the chart at the left to see how the cotton gin affected production.

Cotton Production 1790–1805

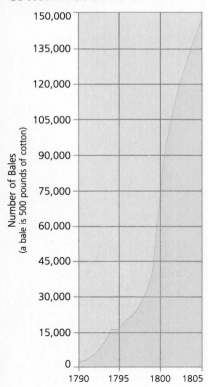

Number of Bales (a bale is 500 pounds of cotton)

SECTION 2 REVIEW

1. Why did England wish to keep plans for its machines secret?
2. Who was Samuel Slater? Eli Whitney?
3. Study the chart at left. About how many bales of cotton were produced in 1790? 1795? 1800? 1805?
4. How do you think the cotton gin affected the production of cotton?
5. Why were Slater and Whitney's machines important?

CHAPTER 13 ACTIVITIES

Wordpower!
In your own words, define each of the listed terms and use each in a sentence.
1. social mobility   2. cotton gin

Reading Skills
This chapter emphasizes social changes, but other kinds also took place. Identify each change listed below as (a) physical, (b) political, or (c) social.
1. The United States became a republic.
2. People could elect their leaders.
3. New lands opened for westward expansion.
4. People could move into a higher class.

Writing Skills
In an essay, the paragraph is the basic unit of thought, and the writer organizes the paragraph in a particular way. The topic sentence, usually first, states the topic of the paragraph and a general idea about that topic. The next few sentences (usually three or four) provide specific evidence—examples, reasons, illustrations, causes, or effects—that explain or support the topic idea. Finally, the writer ends the paragraph with another general sentence that (1) repeats or summarizes the key idea, or (2) states a conclusion that one can draw from the evidence.

Using information from Chapter 13, write a one-paragraph essay that explains some of the social changes in the United States after the Revolution. You may write your own topic sentence or use this one: "After the Revolutionary War, there were many social changes in the United States."

Figure It Out
1. The bar graph at right shows the slave population in the North and South between 1790 and 1820. Study it and answer the questions.
   a. About how many slaves were in the North in 1790? in 1820?

Slave Population in the North and South 1790–1820

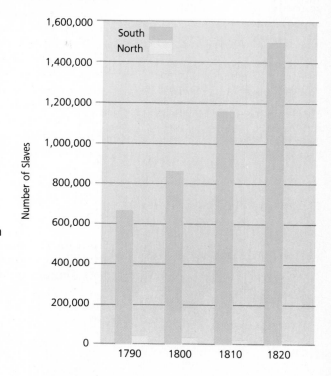

b. About how many slaves were in the South in 1790? in 1820?
c. By studying the graph, what conclusions can you draw about slavery in the United States in this period?
2. Now compare this graph to the graph on the opposite page, which shows cotton production between 1790 and 1805. Keep in mind that (1) cotton grew only in the South, and (2) until the cotton gin was invented, slavery was slowly dying out in both the North and the South. How do you think the cotton gin affected slavery? What evidence supports your answer?

CHAPTER 14

Glossary terms

sparsely   **headwaters**
expedition

Since colonial days, Americans have called four different parts of the country "the West"—land near the Appalachian Mountains, the Mississippi River, the Rocky Mountains, and the Pacific coast. Find each of these four "Wests" on the map below.

Moving West

When most Americans think of "the West," they think of cowboys and Indians, open spaces, and perhaps dusty cattle drives. This is one view of the West, but not the only one.

The United States has, in fact, had four "Wests." To English colonists, land in and near the Appalachian Mountains was the West. After the Revolution, land near the Mississippi River was the West. After 1803, the Rocky Mountains became the West. Today, land along the Pacific coast is the West.

In this chapter, you will mainly study the second West: land near the Mississippi. When Washington became President in 1789, this West was **sparsely** populated, but in the

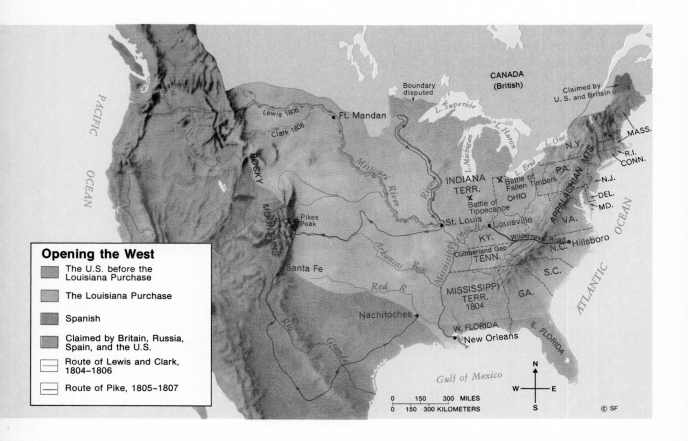

Opening the West

- The U.S. before the Louisiana Purchase
- The Louisiana Purchase
- Spanish
- Claimed by Britain, Russia, Spain, and the U.S.
- Route of Lewis and Clark, 1804–1806
- Route of Pike, 1805–1807

30 years that followed, hundreds of thousands of people moved there. Section 1 looks at trailblazers and explorers who first went west. Section 2 considers population changes. Section 3 looks at frontier life.

SECTION 1 Trailblazers and Explorers

Deciding to go west was one thing. Getting there was another. The Appalachians were like a wall to the early settlers. Someone had to find gaps in the mountains through which people could travel.

Trailblazers in the Second West

The first settlers were people like Daniel Boone. They went west and marked trails for others to follow. Often they followed the network of trails that the eastern Indians had used in trading and in making war. For example, the Indians' Great Warrior Path became the Wilderness Trail, the most widely used settlers' trail. It led through the Cumberland Gap to Kentucky. Thousands of settlers went west on it, turning it into the Wilderness Road. (See map, opposite.)

The first roads were narrow, muddy paths. Wagons often sank into them and could not move. Many people traveled down the Ohio River on flatboats, which looked like floating boxes and carried everything, including cattle. Taking these boats downriver was very dangerous, because steering them was almost impossible.

Exploring the Third West

After Jefferson bought the Louisiana Territory, he wanted it explored. He chose two Virginians, Meriwether Lewis and William Clark, to go beyond the Mississippi into America's third West. Lewis, who was 29 when Jefferson put him in charge of the **expedition,** had been Jefferson's secretary. Clark, then 33, was second in command. He knew the woods well and was a born leader. Jefferson told them to make notes of everything they saw—every Indian tribe, every animal, every plant, every river.

Lewis and Clark chose 30 men to go with them. On the morning of May 14, 1804, they set out from St. Louis, Missouri. For much of the trip, they traveled by boat up the Missouri River. In November, 1804, the men reached a Mandan Indian village in North Dakota, where they built Fort

A mountain man

Reading Skills

Examine the map on the opposite page to decide the following:
1. The boxes in the map key show:
   a. size of areas
   b. ownership of areas
   c. ownership and routes
2. The light and dark shading of the land shows:
   a. ownership of areas
   b. mountains and plains
   c. size of areas

SACAJAWEA
(1787?–1812?)

Sacajawea [sak'ə jə wē'ə] is one of the most honored women in American history. A river and a mountain have been named for her. Yet only a few facts are known about her life.

A member of the Shoshoni tribe, Sacajawea was captured by another tribe in 1800 and sold as a slave to a French Canadian trapper, Toussaint Charbonneau. He married her in 1804.

When Lewis and Clark began exploring the Louisiana Territory, they spent the winter among the Mandan tribe. There they met Charbonneau and Sacajawea, whom they hired as guides.

In February, 1805, Sacajawea gave birth to a son, John, nicknamed Pomp. Two months later, with Pomp strapped to her back, she began guiding the explorers to the Rocky Mountains.

After the expedition ended, she and Charbonneau were hired by another explorer. In 1811, they left Pomp in St. Louis with Clark, because he had offered to educate the boy.

The records of the second expedition say an Indian woman like Sacajawea died in 1812 at a trading post on the Missouri River. However, in 1875 a very old Indian woman named Sacajawea was found among the Shoshoni. She died in 1884.

Mandan and spent the winter. Here they met Sacajawea, a Shoshoni woman who had married a French Canadian trapper. She and her husband joined the expedition as guides.

Clark's slave, York, was able to speak to Sacajawea in French, and so, through him, Lewis and Clark could talk to the Indians. The Indians were friendly to York and amazed by him, for he was the first black man they had ever seen.

In spring, the expedition continued up the Missouri. The explorers saw bears, endless herds of buffalo, elks, bighorn sheep, antelopes, coyotes, and wolves. Unfortunately, they also faced rattlesnakes, insects, and prickly plants.

As they neared the Rocky Mountains, Sacajawea recognized her homeland. She was reunited with her brother, a Shoshoni chief. He helped the men get horses that they used to cross the mountains on what was probably the worst part of the trip. Horses fell down the steep cliffs. When the people ran out of food, they ate their horses and dogs. They reached the Columbia River half-starved.

They made canoes Indian style, by burning out the middle of logs, and paddled down the Columbia to the Pacific Ocean. In the spring, they began the long journey back. For a time, Lewis and Clark separated in order to explore different areas. Arriving in St. Louis in 1806, they found that many people thought they had died. They had traveled 8,000 miles, and their findings spurred western settlement. They had explored the northern part of the Louisiana Territory and beyond, into land claimed by several countries.

In 1805, Jefferson sent Zebulon Pike and 20 men in search of the **headwaters**, or start, of the Mississippi River. They did not find that, but they did make useful records.

In 1806, Pike went into the southern part of the Louisiana Territory, seeking the headwaters of the Arkansas and Red rivers. He and his men found the mountain peak that bears Pike's name. When they found the headwaters of the Rio Grande, they followed the river south into what is now New Mexico, northern Mexico, and Texas.

SECTION 1 REVIEW

1. Why was movement through the Appalachians difficult?
2. What did the Great Warrior Path and the Wilderness Trail have in common?
3. What danger did river travelers face?
4. What was gained by the Lewis and Clark expedition?
5. Where did Zebulon Pike explore?

SECTION 2 Population Movements

The **frontier** was an imaginary line that was nevertheless very real to the people who lived along it. On one side of the line were white and black settlements, on the other, Indian settlements. Study the maps to see how this line moved. Where was the frontier in 1775? In 1820? In 1850?

Glossary terms

frontier
squatter

The Shifting Frontier

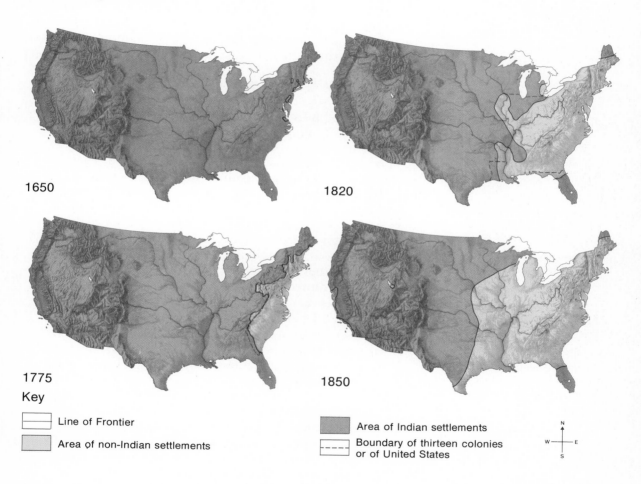

1650

1820

1775

1850

Key

Line of Frontier

Area of non-Indian settlements

Area of Indian settlements

Boundary of thirteen colonies
or of United States

N
W — E
S

The Indians

The first settlers moving west always came into Indian country. The government tried to sign treaties with the Indian tribes to get the rights to their land. Many settlers moved into Indian lands before treaties were signed. The Indians between the Appalachians and the Mississippi River tried to stop them by attacking their settlements. Soldiers fought back. The defeat of several tribes at the Battle of Fallen Timbers in 1794 encouraged American settlement of Ohio.

In the early 1800s, eastern Indians tried once more to stop settlers. The Shawnee leader Tecumseh tried to unite many tribes and defeat the settlers. These efforts ended when Tecumseh was killed during the War of 1812. After that, settlers pushed the Indians farther west.

Who Went West and Why

What types of people moved west? Many kinds, but those who succeeded were strong, healthy, hard-working, and ready to face anything. If they were not, they could not survive. The travel alone tested people's strength.

Many people were poor, but not desperately so. They had enough money to buy a wagon and the oxen to pull it. They also had money for supplies, a guide, or a ride on a boat.

Many bachelors went west. It was easier to travel alone than with a family. If a single man succeeded, he could send "back east" for a bride. Married men sometimes left their families to try to start a better life. Most sent for their families once they were settled, but some never returned. Women who wanted a new life also sometimes ran away from husbands they could not divorce.

The search for better land was a major reason for going west. People got tired of hoeing rocky or worn-out soil. When soil wore out, many people packed up and moved on.

Others went west hoping to become rich by buying land for a low price and then selling it for a higher price. This is called speculation, and sometimes it worked, but sometimes it didn't. Robert Morris, who managed government money during the Revolution, went broke buying western land.

People also went west to get away from high taxes or too many neighbors. In today's terms, the taxes were not very high and the neighbors were not really that close. But to some people in 1800, if you could see the smoke from your neighbor's chimney, you were too close.

A flatboat heads downriver.

Reading Skills

Re-read the last six paragraphs on this page to decide the following about the people who went west:
1. Poor people
   a. few
   b. many
   c. most
2. Married men
   a. few
   b. many
   c. most

The Westward Movement

Historians have seen a pattern to the westward movement. They describe it as taking place in three stages.

Stage 1—hunters and trappers. These were the first white and black men to go west and mark trails. When they returned east, they told stories about plentiful game, green forests, beautiful rivers, and friendly Indians.

Stage 2—pioneers. Pioneers were often poor. Most built crude cabins, kept a few hogs that roamed nearby, planted corn between the stumps of the trees used to build their cabins, and relied upon game for meat. Many did not own the land they farmed. They were **squatters,** people who simply started living on unused land.

Stage 3—settled farmers. These people planned to stay put. They built sturdy houses on land they owned, and they cleared the forest to plant crops. In addition to growing wheat, corn, and other crops, they usually had livestock and went to the trouble to dig a well. They built up their communities, usually building a church first and then a school.

The population of the West grew rapidly, and new states formed following the steps given in the Northwest Ordinance of 1787. The fact that new states were equal to old states encouraged growth.

The lives of settled farmers were far more comfortable than those of pioneers. Fruit orchards and grape arbors took years to establish.

SECTION 2 REVIEW

1. What was the frontier? Where was the frontier in 1775? In 1820? In 1850?
2. Give three reasons that people went west.
3. Which people went west in the first stage of the westward movement? In the second and third stages?
4. Do you think America still has a frontier? Explain your answer.

SECTION 3 Frontier Life

Life on the frontier was farm life. Even those who did not work in the fields often helped farmers. Sawyers cut timber so the farmer could build frame houses and barns. Millers ground wheat into flour and corn into meal. Blacksmiths shoed horses and mended tools. Drovers guided animals to market. Merchants sold salt and cloth to farm families.

What was frontier life like? It **varied.** The stump-filled fields of an Ohio pig farmer offered a different life than the rolling hills of a Kentucky tobacco grower.

Glossary terms

vary
shuck

Farm Making

Clearing land took up much of the life of the first settler. Most frontier farmers had to remove trees and brush, clear stumps, and remove rocks. One person could clear about 15 acres of the heavy forest in a year, not including stumps.

Add the job of providing shelter—first a dugout, then a log cabin, and after some years, if prosperity smiled, a frame home. Add also the building of a barn. Do all this and you still haven't begun the biggest single task for most farmers—fencing. Crops had to be fenced "horse high, bull strong, and hog tight" to keep out animals. A worm fence, which zigged and zagged its way around fields, was most often built.

Felling trees, pulling stumps, building homes, and fencing 40 or 80 acres was huge work. It was done without tractors, chain saws, and pick-up trucks. Yet it was only part of the picture, for crops had to be grown at the same time.

Farm tasks varied depending upon the crop. Tobacco took the most labor. One adult could care for 3 acres at most. On a tobacco farm the people did these tasks:

- In spring, burn off weeds to prepare for seedbeds
- Dig ground and work manure into the soil
- Plant the seed and firm the ground
- In May or June, transplant seedlings to fields
- Weed fields with hoes and plows
- Pull bugs off of *every* leaf of *every* plant *every* week
- Harvest the tobacco: cut, dry, sort, and pack it

Few crops were more demanding on time and backbone. A far less finicky crop was corn. It grew north, south, and west, and it fed America in the 1800s. People ate corn bread, corn pone, mush, hominy, and corn fritters. When fed to hogs, corn became ham, bacon, shanks, chops, and ribs. When fed to cattle and poultry, corn became beef and drumsticks.

Farmers often planted corn between stumps, without plowing, and usually by hand. Scarecrows or children kept birds from eating the young plants. Families prayed to ward off killing frosts. Until corn plants grew taller than weeds—"knee high by the 4th of July"—farm families hoed it.

In the fall, corn didn't require the immediate attention that wheat did when it ripened. Corn was hardy. Farmers cut it at their convenience, put stalks up in "Hallowe'en shocks," and let them dry. Then the family **shucked** (took off the leaves) and shelled the corn by hand. Many a farm son and daughter spent hours and days on this work. Corn-shucking parties with other families made the work fun.

VENERATE THE PLOUGH

Using a horse-drawn plow to turn the soil, a farmer prepares a field for planting.

Socializing

The loneliness of frontier life was hardest for people to bear. Settlers often welcomed travelers just for their company. They let visitors sleep on the floor and shared their food—bread, corn, dried ham, milk, and butter.

Getting together became a popular way to socialize as well as to build houses, make quilts, or attend a wedding. The following is an account of life in Kentucky about 1800.

"Certainly [settlers] never missed a chance for socializing. Just as they made play of corn husking . . . , they also made a "do" of the quilting party, at which the women helped a neighbor line a bedcover. . . .

While the women sewed and [talked], the men indulged in their usual athletics, varied by "plaguing the gals" in the cabin. The gals ate supper first, the men devoting themselves to social drinking, jokes, and horseplay. There was always a lot of singing. . . .

The top social occasion of the backwoods, even more popular than a funeral, was a wedding. The festivities began at the bride's home, and . . . marriages were sometimes postponed until a parson showed up. . . .

By established custom the bride's father set a quart of whisky on his cabin doorstep, and from a mile away the male guests staged a wild horse race to get it. The winner carried it back in triumph to give the groom the first swig.

This drawing of a farm shows a worm fence (on the right), the most common type of fence settlers built.

A quilting bee

Reading Skills

This section uses several figures of speech. What do each of the following mean?
1. Page 28, paragraph 2: "if prosperity smiled"
   a. if people were happy
   b. if people were lucky
2. Page 28, paragraph 5: "demanding on time and backbone"
   a. requiring long, hard work
   b. requiring guts
3. Page 29, paragraph 4: "plaguing the gals"
   a. making the women sick
   b. teasing the women

Both bride and groom were expected to taste at least a little of everything offered to them. . . . The party continued through the night. . . .

The next day there followed the "infare," an entertainment provided by the groom's parents. The guests paired off and rode from the scene of the wedding in a procession led by the bride and groom. The infare had no ceremony connected with it; it was just another night-long party, attesting the endurance of the frontier spirit. But the end was not yet.

The new couple moved to their own cabin on the third day, and that night their friends organized a shivaree [an event] to warm their new house for them. The celebrants arrived in couples, bringing along anything that would [make noise]. Silently they surrounded the cabin. At a signal, shouting, gunfire, pan thumping, and the earthshaking roar of a horse fiddle shattered the silence of the woods. [A horse fiddle was an empty barrel across which the men pulled a fence rail.] That was the start of another party, and for the third time the sun rose on the farewells of the guests. **99**

Parties were the only relief from day after day spent hunting, farming, cooking, and doing many other chores. You can imagine how much settlers looked forward to any party.

SECTION 3 REVIEW
1. Name four steps in making a farm.
2. Which crop required the most time and work? Which was easiest to grow?
3. On what occasions did frontier people get together? Why?

CHAPTER 14 ACTIVITIES

Wordpower!

Unscramble the word in capital letters in each of the sentences below.

1. A place that is PARLYSES populated contains few people.
2. WAHEDASTER are the start of a stream or river.
3. People who did not own land but simply began living on unused land were ATQUERSTS.
4. The NORETIRF was an imaginary line between Indian settlements and white and black settlements.
5. Lewis and Clark formed an IDENOPEXIT to explore the Louisiana Territory.

Reading Skills

Choose the best statement of the relationship between each section and the chapter's title, "Moving West."

Section 1:
   a. purchase of Louisiana Territory
   b. exploring a new region
   c. travels of Lewis and Clark

Section 2:
   a. how people moved
   b. the frontier
   c. roads

Section 3:
   a. starting a farm
   b. going to a wedding
   c. life on the frontier

Writing Skills

Many bachelors went west, found a good location for work and a home, and then sent east for a bride to share pioneer life. Imagine that you're either a bachelor or a possible bride. If you're the bachelor, write a letter persuading a woman to come join you. If you're the bride, write a response to such a letter and include questions you might have about moving west and about life once you get there.

Figure It Out

Lewis and Clark were great explorers but terrible spellers. The drawings and the following account

are from their journals. From the context of the sentences, figure out what the underlined words mean and correct the spelling.

JULY 15, 1805, SUNDAY (Lewis)

Drewyer <u>wonded</u> a deer which ran into the river. My dog pursued, caught it, drowned it, and brought it to shore at our camp. The prickly pear is now in full <u>blume</u> and forms one of the beauties as well as the greatest pests of the plains.

JULY 21, 1805, SUNDAY (Clark)

A fine morning. Our feet so <u>brused</u> and cut that I <u>deturmined</u> to delay for the canoes, & if possible kill some <u>meet</u> by the time they arrived. Small birds are plenty. Some deer, elk, goats, and ibex; no <u>buffalow</u> in the mountains. Those mountains are high and a great <u>perportion</u> of them rocky: <u>Vallies firtile</u>. I observe on the highest <u>pinecals</u> of some of the mountains to the West snow lying in spots. Some still further north are covered with snow and <u>cant</u> be seen from this point.

JULY 22, 1805, MONDAY (Lewis)

Capt. Clark's party had killed a deer and an elk today and ourselves one deer and an antelope only. Altho' Capt. C. was much <u>fatiegued</u> his feet yet blistered and <u>soar</u> he insisted on pursuing his <u>rout</u> in the morning nor <u>weould</u> he consent willingly to my <u>releiving</u> him at that time by taking a tour of the same kind.

UNIT 5 TEST

In your notebook, write the answers to the following questions.

Completion

Fill in each blank with the word that best completes the sentence.

neutral	platform
nationalism	existing
frontier	headwaters
mobility	blockade

1. George Washington told the leaders of England and France that the United States would remain _____, not take sides in their wars.
2. A _____ is a statement of a political party's beliefs and an outline of its programs.
3. England set up a _____ around French ports.
4. _____, or growing pride in America, was one reason for the War of 1812.
5. Social _____ is the ability to move from one social class to another.
6. Pike searched for the _____ of several rivers.
7. The _____ was an imaginary line between Indian lands and lands settled by white and black Americans.

Multiple Choice

Choose the answer that best completes each sentence.
1. Many settlers went west for:
   a. cheap land
   b. more opportunity
   c. both of the above
2. Jefferson did not believe in:
   a. a strict view of the Constitution
   b. the common people's right to have a part in the government
   c. control of the government by the rich

3. Alexander Hamilton did not believe in:
   a. control of the government by the rich
   b. a broad view of the Constitution
   c. the common people's right to control the government
4. Jefferson led this political party:
   a. Federalist
   b. Whig
   c. Republican
5. Hamilton led this political party:
   a. Federalist
   b. Whig
   c. Republican
6. The Louisiana Purchase was important to the United States because:
   a. it doubled the size of the United States
   b. it gave Americans control of the Mississippi River
   c. it gave Americans control of New Orleans
   d. all of the above
7. Reasons for the War of 1812 include all of the following except:
   a. land hunger
   b. desire for freedom of the seas
   c. desire to control France
   d. national pride
8. The three leaders of explorations in the Louisiana Territory were:
   a. Jefferson, Hamilton, and Madison
   b. Lewis, Clark, and Pike
   c. Kraig, Greer, and Roden
9. Which of the following was not a result of the War of 1812?
   a. the United States was more independent
   b. the United States gained Canada and Spain
   c. the United States became more industrial
10. People who simply settled on unused land were:
    a. settled farmers
    b. squatters
    c. explorers

11. Farmers in western Pennsylvania rebelled because of the excise tax on:
    a. corn
    b. wheat
    c. whiskey
12. Tecumseh dreamed of:
    a. making Indiana a state
    b. persuading Indians not to fight American settlers
    c. forming a confederation of the eastern Indian tribes

Tricky Questions

If a statement is true, write "True" next to its number. If a statement is false, correct it to make it true.

1. The United States changed very little between 1787 and 1815.
2. Few people had a chance to advance their social positions in the United States.
3. Between 1787 and 1815, the ideas of equality and democracy grew.
4. All people had a chance to improve their lives between 1787 and 1815.
5. The frontier moved further westward between 1787 and 1815.
6. Cheap land played a part in social mobility during this period.
7. Eli Whitney invented the cotton gin in 1793.
8. Samuel Slater was the man responsible for the first cotton mill in the United States.
9. The cotton gin had no effect on the production of cotton in the South.
10. The absence of nobility in the United States made it easier to become a member of the upper class.

Essay

Washington, Hamilton, and Jefferson influenced important decisions that shaped the United States for many years. Which *one* of these men do you believe had the most effect on shaping the country? Give your opinion, and explain three or four reasons for your choice in a one-paragraph essay.

Reading Graphic Aids

Identify the places numbered on the map. Each place is described below.
1. capital of the United States
2. mountains that the first settlers crossed to go West
3. major trail west
4. an important port gained through the Louisiana Purchase
5. major river that the United States began to control through the Louisiana Purchase
6. river used by Lewis and Clark
7. country north of the United States
8. state that entered the Union in 1792

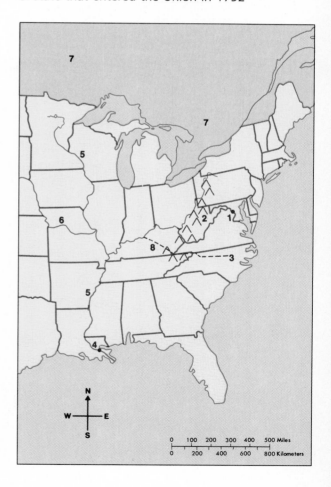

UNIT 6

Fourth of July celebration in Philadelphia, 1819

A GROWING NATION

1815–1850

It is very easy to study the period from 1815 to 1850 and come away with the idea that Andrew Jackson, Henry Clay, and a few other men *were* American history at this time. Yet, this is a mistake, for these leaders were political stars in Washington, D.C. To know *who* America was, and *how* America was living, you must look beyond Washington and into the city streets, small towns, and farmlands. When you do this, you find some surprises.

First, if you are doing your looking in 1820, you see many children. In that year, half of all Americans are 16 or younger. Second, half the people are female. This fact isn't shocking, but it is often overlooked. Third, one sixth are black, most, but not all, in slavery in the South. If you can't see or hear many immigrants speaking different languages, just wait a few years. If you don't see many Indians, don't strain your eyes. They've either died or are soon to be forced to move farther west.

And what are these Americans doing? Well, three quarters of them are farming, which isn't easy work. Manufacturing, mining, fishing, whaling, and other work account for the rest.

Looking at how Americans worked doesn't tell all. They also sang, learned to read, worshipped, and died. They dated, married, and had children. Above all, they lived in their own present. They had no more idea that a Civil War was coming in 40 years, or an automobile in 80, than Americans today know what will happen in 2030 or 2070.

In this unit, you will study American life and politics between 1815 and 1850. You will see who Americans elected, how Americans lived and worked, what they thought, and how different sections of the country began to develop very different ways of life.

TIME LINE

1805

1807   *Clermont* makes first successful steamboat trip

1810

1811   Work begun on National Road

1812–1814   War of 1812

1817–1825   Era of Good Feelings

The *Clermont*, America's first steamboat, invented by Robert Fulton

1820

1822   Cotton mills open at Lowell, Massachusetts

1823   Erie Canal completed

1824   Caucus system ends

1826   American Temperance Society forms

Boat on the Erie Canal

1828   Two-party election

1829   Andrew Jackson becomes President

1830   1830   Indian Removal Act

General Andrew Jackson hero of the Battle of Ne Orleans, 1814

1836   First woman's college opens

1837   First state board of education

1840

1843–1847   Irish potato crop failures

1844   Morse demonstrates telegraph

1848   Woman's rights convention in Seneca Falls, New York

1850

1854   Know-Nothing party forms

Primary school in New York, 1825

CHAPTER 15

Politics and Reform

Between 1815 and 1850, politics changed greatly. For a few years, the country had only one major political party. Then Americans formed two parties. They also changed the rules for choosing candidates and let more people vote.

Many Americans also began changing their views of what government should do. Groups of people began urging state governments to open public schools, take care of the mentally ill, and give women the same legal rights as men.

This chapter is about these changes. Section 1 describes party politics. Section 2 is about several reform movements.

SECTION 1 Party Politics

Soon after President James Monroe took office in 1817, he visited New England. Monroe was a Virginia Republican and a follower of Jefferson. Although Federalists in New England had been against other Republican Presidents, they greeted Monroe in a friendly way. A Boston newspaper said that his inauguration had begun an "era of good feelings." For that reason, the period from 1817 to about 1825 is called the Era of Good Feelings. Political feelings seemed good on the surface because the Federalist party had almost disappeared and no strong second party opposed the Republicans. Behind the scenes, however, was a good deal of disagreement. Increasing democracy was one reason.

Increasing Democracy

In the Era of Good Feelings, politics became more democratic. The constitutions of new states forming in the West, unlike those in the East, let most men vote. They also let voters choose presidential electors and many state officials.

These increases in democracy made political parties more important. Parties wrote platforms that voters could favor or oppose. They also provided organizations that could elect or defeat candidates. However, voters had no voice in choosing the parties' candidates for office. Party leaders in **caucuses**, or party meetings, chose the nominees. In 1820, the Federalist party had no caucus because it had almost no members.

Glossary terms

caucus	**rotation in office**
suffrage	**spoils system**
corrupt	

To reach the many new voters, politicians traveled around giving speeches.

ANDREW JACKSON
(1767–1845)

When historians make lists of the greatest Presidents, Andrew Jackson is always near the top because he was a truly strong President.

The son of farmer parents in the Carolinas, Jackson's early years were poor and hard. As a boy of 13, he fought against the English in the Revolution. Captured, he was put in a prison camp where he caught smallpox.

An orphan at 14, Jackson had to make his way in the world. He began to study law and served in the militia of Tennessee. He became a judge and a landowner with many slaves. As a general in the War of 1812, his defeat of the English at New Orleans made him a national hero. Jackson was so powerful and tough that people called him "Old Hickory" after that knotty, hard tree.

Jackson's ideas were simple: Americans should be free to make their own ways in the world. He hated anything that got in their way—banks, rich people, the federal government, or Indians. By the time Jackson died, he had seen America grow from 13 colonies on the Atlantic coast to a huge nation. He had much to do with this growth.

The choice of the Republican caucus, President James Monroe, ran for a second term without opposition.

As the 1824 election drew near, some people opposed using a caucus to name a candidate because whoever the Republican caucus nominated would become President. To many, this idea seemed unfair and undemocratic. They thought the voters should have a voice in choosing candidates.

The Election of 1824

In 1824, a caucus met, but only a third of the Republican leaders attended. They nominated William H. Crawford of Georgia for President. Republicans in the state legislatures or at large meetings chose three other candidates—Andrew Jackson, Henry Clay, and John Quincy Adams.

In the election, no candidate won a majority of the electoral votes. Therefore, the House of Representatives had to choose between Jackson and Adams, the leading candidates. Jackson had received more popular votes and more electoral votes than Adams. However, Clay asked his supporters to vote for Adams, and so the House elected Adams.

After taking office, Adams chose Clay to be Secretary of State, a job that most Americans viewed as training to be President. Jackson's angry followers charged that Clay and Adams had made a dirty deal. They said Clay made Adams President in 1824 because Adams promised to make Clay President later. Jackson's backers were determined to win in 1828, and they began getting ready.

Two Parties

By 1828, the country again had two parties. Some Republicans picked up many Federalist ideas and called themselves National Republicans. They supported Adams for reelection. The Republicans backed by farmers in the South and West called themselves Democratic-Republicans or Democrats. Claiming to be the true followers of Jefferson, they chose Andrew Jackson as their candidate.

The 1828 campaign was a dirty grudge fight. Jackson's backers accused Adams of waste and various crimes as President. Adams's supporters accused Jackson of even worse crimes, including murder. The charges against both men were false, but they brought voters to the polls in great numbers. Jackson easily defeated Adams.

Jackson was the first President elected under the new **suffrage**, or voting, laws that let all white men over the age

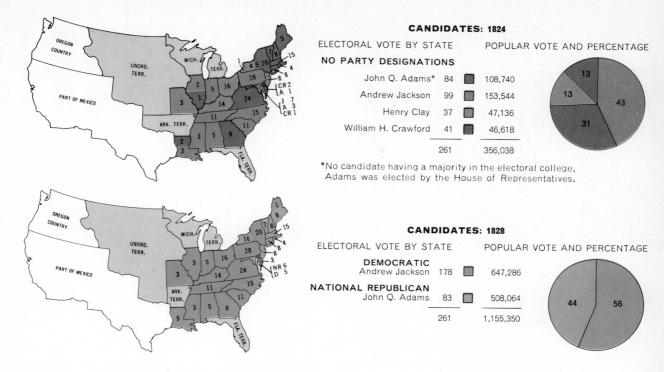

CANDIDATES: 1824

ELECTORAL VOTE BY STATE

POPULAR VOTE AND PERCENTAGE

NO PARTY DESIGNATIONS

John Q. Adams*	84		108,740
Andrew Jackson	99		153,544
Henry Clay	37		47,136
William H. Crawford	41		46,618
	261		356,038

*No candidate having a majority in the electoral college, Adams was elected by the House of Representatives.

CANDIDATES: 1828

ELECTORAL VOTE BY STATE

POPULAR VOTE AND PERCENTAGE

DEMOCRATIC

Andrew Jackson	178		647,286

NATIONAL REPUBLICAN

John Q. Adams	83		508,064
	261		1,155,350

of 21 vote. Voters no longer had to own property.

The growth of the Democratic party was an important part of a new spirit of democracy under Jackson. Jackson and his followers based their party on strong local organizations in large states such as New York and Virginia. They put on a big election campaign with parades, signs, newspapers, and advertisements. They said that Jackson, the war hero, represented the common people of America and that his opponents were rich and **corrupt**, or morally bad.

The Democratic party did so well in 1828 among working people and farmers that other parties copied its methods. In 1832, the National Republican party—renamed the Whig party—accused Jackson of being a king. The Whigs tried to show that they represented the common people by holding a convention at which delegates chosen by voters named the party's candidates. The Democrats soon followed the Whigs' example and began choosing candidates at conventions.

Now in every election each side fought for votes. In the 1840 campaign, free liquor flowed, and promises flowed even more freely. This age of rough-and-tumble politics was the style of the new democracy begun by Andrew Jackson.

Study the electoral charts above. What part of the country supported Adams in 1824? What part supported the National Republicans in 1828? Where did Jackson pick up the support needed to win in 1828?

WHY WHIG?

The Whig party in England backed the American colonists before the Revolution and opposed the Tory laws that led Americans to revolt. By taking the name *Whig*, the National Republicans hoped to link themselves to an old pro-American memory.

On election day, voters announced their choices in public—there was no secret ballot. The backers of each candidate cheered and drank toasts as the vote totals rose.

Jackson claimed to speak for most Americans. He believed that if people stayed in public office too long, they became corrupt. He believed in **rotation in office**—moving officials from one job to another, or to none at all, in a regular way. What better way than by elections?

Jackson also thought that all free men should be able to vote and hold any public office. Since Jackson believed that the average man could handle any government job, he also favored the **spoils system.** That is, he thought the people who worked to elect a party's candidates should be rewarded with government jobs. He liked the old Roman saying about war: "To the victor goes the spoils." As President, he fired many government workers and put loyal Democrats into their jobs. Later Presidents followed his lead in hiring and firing government workers according to party.

Reading Skills

Read the first paragraph on this page and identify each numbered item below as one of the following:
a. statement of Jackson's idea
b. definition of his idea
c. his reason for believing the idea
d. other

1. People who stay in public office too long become corrupt.
2. rotation in office
3. moving officials from one job to another

SECTION 1 REVIEW

1. Why was the "Era of Good Feelings" called by that name?
2. Why did the caucus system end?
3. How was John Quincy Adams elected President in 1824?
4. What party did the National Republicans replace? What name did the National Republican party take in the 1830s?
5. Which parts of the country backed the Democratic-Republicans?
6. In what ways did Jackson and his followers change the Democratic party?
7. How did the Whigs change election campaigns?
8. How did Jackson change the way of hiring and firing government workers?

SECTION 2 Reform Movements

In the early 1800s, some Americans wanted to **reform** society. They thought people could improve their lives if society changed. They formed groups that demanded social reforms, often asking state governments to provide new services.

Children, Education, and Work

Children were a big concern for many reformers. In the 1830s, reformers began to demand that states set up free public schools. Many people wanted the growing numbers of new voters to be well enough educated to make thoughtful voters. Also, many Americans viewed school as a good place to teach immigrants American ways.

The first board of education appeared in Massachusetts in 1837, headed by Horace Mann, who organized a statewide system of free public schools. Public and private schools grew in number in all states. By 1860, about 80 percent of white boys and girls in the North between the ages of 10 and 14 attended school at some time. Many free black children attended school, but they were **segregated**, that is, placed in separate schools.

For many students, the school "year" was less than two months because work came first. Children started work about age 12. Most farm boys attended school only in winter, and apprentices in cities also had short school years.

Grade school was the end for most students. In 1860, there were only 300 high schools in the whole country. Girls finished school at 15. Some boys remained in grade school until 19 because work constantly interrupted their education.

In the early 1800s, only 20 percent of American women lived to see their youngest child become an adult, and there were many more orphans than today. They lived with relatives, in poorhouses set up by churches, or, if apprentices, with their masters. Some reformers pushed to set up orphanages.

Women and Their Rights

Many reformers were women. When they found that their lack of political power kept them from winning some reforms, they began a campaign to get more rights.

In the 1800s, women had few legal rights. They could not vote or hold office. If they married, their husbands had complete power over them. If a woman inherited property, in

reform
segregate
temperance
abolitionist

Young women attending an evening school

M. & M. Korolik Collection, Museum of Fine Arts, Boston

ELIZABETH CADY STANTON
(1815–1902)

The fact that American women today have many legal rights is largely the result of the work of a woman from Johnstown, New York—Elizabeth Cady Stanton.

Young Elizabeth never had happy memories of her parents, who were very strict people. She did have a friend in the family minister. He encouraged her to study hard, and under his guidance she graduated from one of the first women's high schools in 1832.

Although women could not become lawyers, she studied law. After she married and had six children, she became a crusader for equal rights.

Stanton joined forces with men and women with similar ideas. They met in 1848 at Seneca Falls, New York. There they drew up a statement saying that men and women were equal and that women should have the right to vote.

Many Americans laughed at their ideas, but that did not stop Stanton. With other leaders, she spent the next 50 years working toward these goals. She wrote many articles and books, and she spoke everywhere.

The fight was long and hard. But by the time she died, some of her goals had been won.

most cases when she married it became her husband's property. If a woman took a job, her pay went to her husband.

How did women fit into society? In the early 1800s, most women married, and they married between the ages of 18 and 22. Single women could move more freely than married women, and some single women dated without chaperones.

Between 1800 and 1830, marriage began to be based on love. This had not always been true. Many colonists had not married for love. Many marriages were arranged by families, and a couple might marry as strangers.

During the early 1800s, women began having fewer babies. Even with smaller families, child and home care were huge jobs. No indoor toilets, no running water, and no easy-to-reach doctor made child rearing hard. Many women also worked in the fields at busy times, often while pregnant.

This rather dark picture is broken by some light. Around 1840, for the first time in American history, wives could expect to live longer than their husbands. With fewer babies, not as many women died giving birth. Also, education for women became more available. Colleges for women opened beginning in 1836. Many women became teachers—the first in Mississippi in 1839.

Still, women faced many barriers. They could not speak in public, even about religion. They could not become lawyers. The first woman doctor in the United States, Elizabeth Blackwell, finished medical school in 1849 only after years of working to be admitted.

With society changing so much, some women demanded their rights as humans. In 1848, Elizabeth Cady Stanton and Lucretia Mott organized a woman's rights convention in New York. They demanded the right to vote and the right to control their own property and wages.

Temperance

Another concern of reformers was drinking. Americans had long been hard drinkers, in part because good water was hard to find. Rum, beer, whiskey, and hard apple cider were the most common alcoholic drinks. By the 1820s, many reformers began to see drink as an evil that broke up homes and brought on poverty.

In 1826, the American Temperance Society was founded. It had two main goals: (1) to persuade people to "take the pledge" and promise not to drink alcohol, and (2) to urge states to pass laws against the sale or drinking of alcohol.

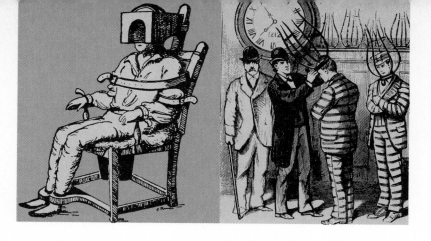

Both prisoners and the mentally ill were treated harshly. Mentally ill people might be strapped into chairs (left). Prisoners might be made to wear a metal head cage (middle). Dorothea Dix (below) worked to help both these groups of people.

Temperance groups put on big campaigns urging Americans to stop drinking. Many thousands swore off anything stronger than lemonade. By 1855, laws in 13 states prevented the sale or drinking of liquors. In many states, however, these laws were so unpopular they were later repealed.

Other Reforms

Reformers worked in many other areas. For example, Dorothea Dix, a Boston schoolteacher, tried to improve the treatment of the mentally ill. She traveled many thousands of miles to urge state governments to build decent places for these people. Later, Dix worked for prison reform.

Some reformers formed new communities in which people tried to live and work in cooperation and friendship. In places like New Harmony, Indiana, the community as a whole owned all property.

In sum, many reforms helped Americans adjust to change. They helped round off the hard edges of a rough new society. But, as you shall see later, one movement did not simply want to improve American life. **Abolitionists**—people who opposed slavery—wanted to break up a way of life they saw as evil.

SECTION 2 REVIEW

1. At what ages did most children (a) start work, and (b) finish school?
2. Which state had the first free public schools?
3. What were the goals of the American Temperance Society?
4. What rights did Stanton and Mott think women should have?
5. Who led the fight to reform institutions for the mentally ill?
6. What do you think was happening in the early 1800s that made people so interested in making society and people better?

Reading Skills

Writers use different methods to explain and illustrate the topics of paragraphs. They use (1) examples or descriptive details, (2) reasons, and (3) actions or events. Re-read the three paragraphs on page 42, beginning with "This rather dark . . .". Decide which method is the main one used in each paragraph to explain and illustrate.

CHAPTER 15 ACTIVITIES

Wordpower!

In your own words, define each of the terms listed below and use it in a sentence.

caucus   segregate
suffrage   reform
spoils system   temperance

Reading Skills

This chapter is about changes of two kinds. Which kinds of changes does the chapter describe?

1. Political and economic
2. Political and social
3. Social and economic

Writing Skills

At the time public schools appeared, the relationship between children and adults was more formal than it is today. In letters, children often sent their "duty" to their parents rather than their love. Laws required children to show parents respect and behave properly. By the mid-1800s, American ideas about children changed. Physical punishment by parents, such as "tanning" with a switch, became less common. School practices, such as "sitting on the wall" (squatting on air against the wall), slowly disappeared. People thought moral stories would do more to improve behavior.

Imagine you are living in 1840. Write a short letter to an adult explaining how you think teachers should treat their pupils.

Figure It Out

Study the table below and answer these questions.

1. In which southern state did the largest percentage of white men vote in 1824? In 1840?
2. In which state did the percentage of voters increase the most between 1824 and 1840?
3. In which state did the percentage of voters increase the least between 1824 and 1840?
4. In what states did the majority of adults vote? Explain your answer.
5. What would be a good title for this chart?

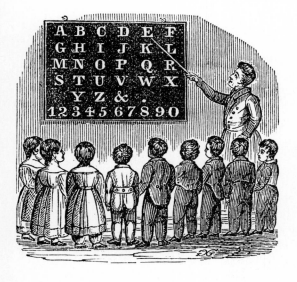

Voter Participation 1824–1840*

South	1824	1828	1832	1836	1840
Delaware	—	—	67.0	69.4	82.8
Maryland	53.7	76.2	55.6	67.5	84.6
Virginia	11.5	27.6	30.8	35.0	54.6
North Carolina	42.2	56.8	31.7	52.9	83.1
Georgia	—	35.9	33.0	64.9	88.9
Kentucky	25.3	70.7	73.9	61.1	74.3
Tennessee	26.8	49.8	28.8	55.2	89.6
Louisiana	—	36.3	24.4	19.2	39.4
Alabama	52.1	53.6	33.3	65.0	89.8
Mississippi	41.6	56.6	32.8	62.8	88.2
Arkansas	—	—	—	35.0	86.4

*Percentage of white men, 21 and over, voting in presidential elections. No figures are given for South Carolina because voters did not choose presidential electors in that state in these elections. —No figures available.

CHAPTER 16

The Growth of Sections

Abraham Lincoln and Jefferson Davis were born 8 months and 96 miles apart into frontier farm families in Kentucky.

The Davises went southwestward to Louisiana and then to Mississippi. They began to plant cotton and buy slaves.

The Lincoln family moved to Indiana and then to Illinois. They continued to farm a small piece of land. Lincoln grew up in one section, the Northwest, Davis in another, the South.

A **section** is a large area in which the people think and work alike. The boundaries of a section are vague and likely to change. However, between 1815 and 1850, the United States had three main sections: the Northeast, the Northwest, and the South, shown on the map below. Life began to differ greatly in these parts of the United States. These changes led to **sectionalism**—a feeling of loyalty to a section. Section 1 of the text describes the Northeast. Section 2 deals with the South. Section 3 is about the Northwest.

This map shows how the United States was divided into sections in the years before 1850. What states were in the Northeast? The South? The Northwest?

Sections, 1815–1850

- Northeast
- South
- Northwest
- 1816 Date state entered the Union

0   100   200   300 Miles
0   200   400 Kilometers

Map: Sections, 1815–1850

CANADA

L. Superior
L. Michigan
L. Huron
L. Ontario
L. Erie

VERMONT 1791
MAINE 1820
NEW HAMPSHIRE 1788
MASSACHUSETTS 1788
RHODE ISLAND 1790
CONNECTICUT 1788
NEW JERSEY 1787
DELAWARE 1787
MARYLAND 1788

MICHIGAN 1837
WISCONSIN 1848
NEW YORK 1788
PENNSYLVANIA 1787
IOWA 1846
INDIANA 1816
OHIO 1803
ILLINOIS 1818
MISSOURI 1821
VIRGINIA 1788
KENTUCKY 1792
TENNESSEE 1796
NORTH CAROLINA 1789
ARKANSAS 1836
SOUTH CAROLINA 1788
MISSISSIPPI 1817
ALABAMA 1819
GEORGIA 1788
TEXAS 1845
LOUISIANA 1812
FLORIDA 1845

ATLANTIC OCEAN

Gulf of Mexico

N
W   E
S

45

SECTION 1 The Northeast

In both 1815 and 1850, most of the people in the Northeast made a living by farming. However, great changes had begun that would continue after 1850. One way to learn how the Northeast changed is to study the table and chart below.

Occupations in the Northeast 1840

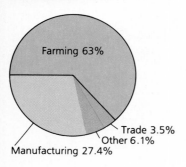

Farming 63%

Trade 3.5%
Other 6.1%
Manufacturing 27.4%

Urban-Rural Population in the Northeast 1820–1850

	Total	Rural	Urban	Percent urban
1820	4,360,000	3,880,000	480,000	11
1830	5,542,000	4,758,000	785,000	14
1840	6,761,000	5,508,000	1,253,000	19
1850	8,627,000	6,338,000	2,289,000	27

Changes in Farming

One thing the table does not show is that during the 1830s, farmers in many parts of the Northeast faced hard times. Their land had been farmed so long the soil had worn out, and farmers could not raise grain or animals cheaply enough to compete with farms in Ohio, Indiana, and Illinois.

These farmers had two choices: (1) they could leave their poor land, or (2) they could stay put but produce different crops. Thousands of northeastern farmers left their farms. In the Northeast as a whole, however, most farmers stayed on their farms. They began producing crops that the growing cities needed but could not easily get from a distance—milk, butter, cheese, potatoes, fruit, and hay.

Making butter for sale

Manufacturing

For the Northeast, the biggest change was the growth of manufacturing. In 1815, most manufacturing took place in small shops and mills or in the home itself. By 1850 the use of steam-powered machines and better transportation had changed this.

Factories developed in New England in the cotton industry. Two different systems began. One hired entire families. Children as young as 4 or 5 helped tend the machines. Workers lived in rooms in large brick buildings called **tenements** in the factory towns.

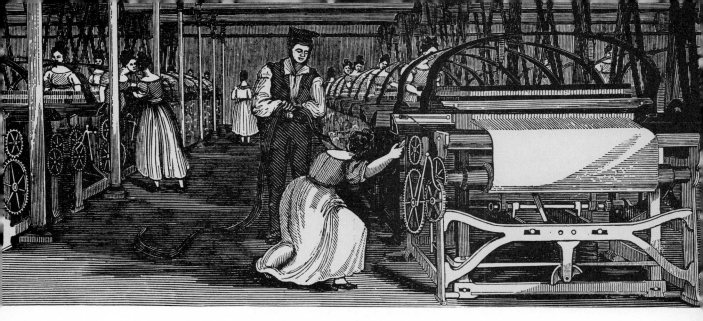

Weavers in a cotton mill

The other developed in the cotton mills of Lowell, Massachusetts. The Lowell owners hired young farm women, housed them in **dormitories**, and carefully supervised them. The workers dressed in white, and, despite long working hours and a 10 p.m. bedtime, had time to read, go to lectures, and print a newspaper. These practices were so unusual that they were called the "Lowell experiment."

The Lowell women were single and between the ages of 15 and 25. They were expected to quit upon marrying. Pay was $2.50 to $3.00 a week, from which $1.25 was deducted for living costs. As many as eight women slept in each small room.

Cities

The number of cities grew rapidly in this period. A few large cities—New York, Philadelphia, and Boston—could trace their growth to trade. However, most cities in the Northeast grew because they were manufacturing centers. In their factories, raw materials from many different places were brought together. Using machines powered by water or steam, workers turned them into finished goods.

Both immigrants and farm people searching for factory jobs caused city populations to swell. Most immigrants landed at New York, Boston, and Philadelphia, and they generally stayed in those cities or moved nearby. After 1840, growing numbers of immigrants from Ireland and Germany arrived.

Hours of Work Cotton Mills

	Summer	Winter
Start	5 a.m.	7 a.m.
Breakfast	7:30–8:00	Before work
Dinner	12:30–1:15	12:30–1:00
Quitting	7 p.m.	7 p.m.

Even at Lowell, workers put in more than 70 hours, six days a week.

Reading Skills

To understand history, you need to separate cause and effect. In each pair below, which is the <u>cause</u> and which is the <u>effect</u>?

1. worn-out soil/hard times for northeastern farmers
2. change to different crops/poor land
3. development of factories/steam-powered machines

Glossary term

overseer

Occupations in the South 1840

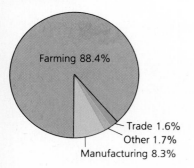

Farming 88.4%

Trade 1.6%
Other 1.7%
Manufacturing 8.3%

SECTION 1 REVIEW

1. What percent of northeasterners lived in cities in 1820? In 1850?
2. In which decade did the urban population grow the most?
3. Next to farmers, what was the largest category for white male workers in 1840?
4. What were wages, hours, and working conditions in the Lowell cotton mills?
5. Figuring the usual six-day week, how many hours a week did the average mill worker put in during the summer? In the winter? Allowing eight hours for sleep, how many free hours did workers have in the summer before or after work?
6. How did manufacturing affect northeastern cities?
7. How did immigration affect the Northeast?

SECTION 2 The South

The biggest change in the South between 1815 and 1850 was from one kind of farming to another. After the War of 1812, cotton grown on plantations became the leading crop.

The South, however, was not made up of cotton plantations alone. Tobacco, sugar, and rice plantations also existed, all of them worked by slaves. Countless small farms produced still other crops. Farm owners, not slaves, worked them. But cotton made much more money than any other southern crop. Cotton and slavery, more than anything else, made the South different from other sections. Study the chart and table to see where and how southerners lived and worked.

Where and Who

Tobacco, cotton, and corn were hard on the soil. In the older states along the Atlantic coast, growing these crops year after year wore out the soil. Also, heavy rains washed

Urban-Rural Population in the South 1820–1850

	Total	Rural	Urban	Percent urban
1820	4,419,000	4,216,000	204,000	5
1830	5,708,000	5,407,000	301,000	5
1840	6,951,000	6,488,000	463,000	7
1850	8,983,000	8,239,000	744,000	8

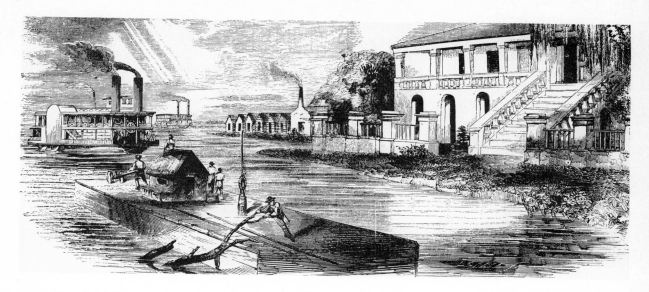

away much of the richest dirt. Many southeastern farmers abandoned their worn-out lands and moved west.

The earliest settlers in places like Alabama and Mississippi owned small farms and had no slaves. As time passed, some of them bought slaves and more land while others sold out, moved farther west, and pioneered again. Also, planters from the eastern states moved in with slaves and money.

Books and movies have painted a romantic picture of the Old South. It includes big houses, great fields, smiling servants, singing field hands, and friendly white gentlemen and ladies. But in the real South, most people were neither slaves nor slaveholders. Most white southerners were neither rich nor poor. They lived on family-owned farms and had no slaves. Some hired a slave or two to help in busy seasons. About 37 percent of the population was black. All but a very few blacks were slaves. Planters who owned huge fields and big beautiful houses made up less than 1 percent of the white population. However, they controlled most of the wealth of the South. They also led in politics. Among these planters, those who grew cotton were more influential than those who grew tobacco, sugar cane, or rice.

Slaves at Work

On large plantations, slaves did most of the work. Some worked at crafts or in the house, but most were field hands.

How well slaves and slaveholders got along depended

This old drawing shows a planter's house and sugar plantation built on the bank of the Mississippi River. Slave cabins are in the background. Plantation owners tried to build near a waterway so that boats could tie up at the plantation dock and carry crops away.

An overseer directing slave work

upon the individuals. Some developed close personal ties. Members of a slaveholding family might work alongside their slaves. Other slaveholders treated slaves as slaves.

Most slaveholders were careful to protect their own interests when using slaves. For example, they seldom had slaves dig ditches in swamps or catch cotton bales on docks. They hired immigrants for such dangerous work. If a slave died, the slaveholder lost "property" worth $1,000 or more. If a hired hand died, the employer lost nothing.

The slaveholder hired an **overseer,** generally a white man, who grouped the field workers into gangs. Each gang was led by a male slave called the "driver." He carried a whip that he used, if necessary, to keep the gang on the move. The larger the crop, the larger the overseer's pay. Overseers therefore tried to get as much work as possible out of slaves.

Slaves did almost all the work of raising cotton. About 60 percent of American slaves in 1850 worked at this job.

Southern Cities

The South had some industries and a few large cities. Shortly after the War of 1812, many southerners talked of building cotton mills to take advantage of the section's water power and raw material. Because cotton-raising made more money than cotton-milling, only a few mills were built in the South. Instead, southern cities concentrated on trade.

Most of the cotton, tobacco, rice, and sugar bound for the North or for Europe went through Baltimore, Norfolk, Richmond, Charleston, Savannah, or New Orleans. These important seaports had banks, warehouses, and merchants' offices for carrying on trade.

Cities next to waterfalls had the water power needed for factories. Birmingham, Columbia, and Raleigh owed part of their growth to their location near rivers with falls. Using water power, workers sawed logs into lumber, milled grain into flour, and made turpentine from pine sap.

SECTION 2 **REVIEW**

1. What became the main southern crop after the War of 1812?
2. How did most southerners make a living between 1815 and 1850?
3. What percentage of southerners were black? What percentage of southerners owned big houses and great fields?
4. Why did southerners favor cotton-growing over cotton-milling?
5. What were the main businesses in southern cities?

50

SECTION 3 The Agricultural Northwest

Glossary terms

survey
grain drill
reaper

Between 1815 and 1850, the Northwest was very much a land of farms and farmers. Some cities grew as centers of industry and trade, but farming remained most important. Most people lived and worked on farms of about 200 acres.

Land laws encouraged settlement. As the government **surveyed** each new piece of public land, it opened land offices and sold the land to the highest bidders. After the War of 1812, pioneers rushed west to take up land. At this time, a person had to pay the government at least $2 an acre and buy at least 160 acres. However, in 1820, Congress changed the law. It lowered the starting price to $1.25 and the smallest purchase to 80 acres. Now with as little as $100 in cash, a person could buy land for a farm.

Most people who went west from Pennsylvania, Maryland, Virginia, North Carolina, Kentucky, and Tennessee traveled down the Ohio River. They settled in the southern parts of Ohio, Indiana, and Illinois—the parts that were occupied earliest. People from New England or New York or Boston usually came west by way of the Great Lakes. They settled in the northern parts of Ohio, Indiana, and Illinois, as well as in Michigan and Wisconsin. Study the chart and table to see where people lived and how they worked.

Urban-Rural Population in the Northwest 1820–1850

	Total	Rural	Urban	Percent urban
1820	859,000	850,000	10,000	1
1830	1,610,000	1,569,000	42,000	3
1840	3,352,000	3,222,000	129,000	4
1850	5,404,000	4,904,000	499,000	9

Occupations in the Northwest 1840

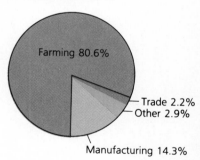

Farming 80.6%
Trade 2.2%
Other 2.9%
Manufacturing 14.3%

Making a Farm

Many parts of the Northwest were almost unbroken forest. A visitor wrote: "The entire country is still nothing but one huge forest in which they have carved out some clearings. When you climb a steeple, as far as you can see are the tops of trees, which the wind moves like the waves of the sea."

A farmer sows seed by hand on the flat grasslands of Illinois.

New machines like this one increased the size of crops.

Another large part of the Northwest was treeless and covered with wild grass. The pioneers had never seen anything quite like this grass, in some places as tall as a person. They avoided it because the roots of the grass were hard to plow. Plowing became easier and faster after 1819, when iron plows replaced wooden ones. Before long, determined settlers began to plow the grassland, growing big crops in the rich black soil. About 1830, steel plows became available. They cut the soil more cleanly and deeply and lasted even longer than iron plows.

Other machines helped increase farm production. Horse-drawn **grain drills** made planting easier. Mowing machines and hay rakes improved harvesting. Finally, in 1831, Cyrus H. McCormick developed a machine called a **reaper.** Using his reaper, a crew of 6 or 7 workers could harvest as much in a day as 15 workers using old-fashioned tools.

These machines were used most in the Northwest for three reasons. (1) Many farmers there could afford them. (2) The land was flat enough for easy use of the machines. (3) Grain fields were big enough to make machine use economical.

At first, most farms in the Northwest produced crops only for the use of the farm family. Later, they began to specialize in certain crops and produce them for sale. The chief products became corn, wheat, pork, and beef.

Cities

The cities of the Northwest developed differently from those in the Northeast. At first, they were shipping and storing centers for goods from farms and forests. As time passed, they became processing centers as well. In the cities, workers cut logs into lumber and turned lumber into furniture. Flour-milling, meat-packing, whiskey-distilling, and leather-tanning all became important industries. Later, factories that made farm tools appeared.

How fast a city grew depended upon its location and resources. Cincinnati was in a good spot to make furniture, tools, clocks, and other things used daily. Its factories supplied most states west of the Appalachians. So many pigs were slaughtered there—about 150,000 a year—that people called the city "Porkopolis."

Slaughtered pigs and manufactured goods left Cincinnati by boat on the Ohio River and other waterways. St. Louis, on the Mississippi River, and Chicago, on Lake Michigan, also became major port cities in the Northwest.

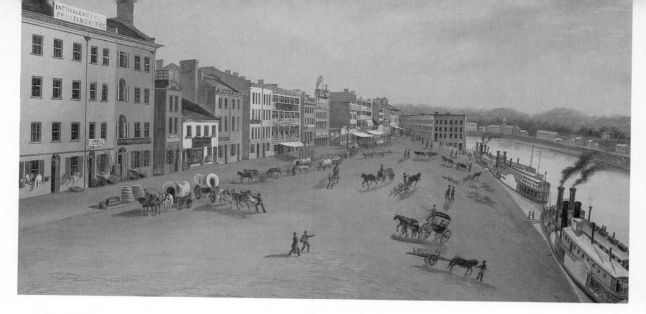

The Cincinnati waterfront in 1835

When Chicago became a town in 1833, it contained 150 houses and one hotel. It grew rapidly, in part because of its location on Lake Michigan. Shipping goods and people by boat was the fastest means of transportation at this time. It also was, and still is, the cheapest way to move bulky goods like grain.

At Chicago, many pioneers heading west switched from boats to wagons. In summer, parties of pioneers went through daily. A visitor described them as "wild, rough, almost savage-looking men from North Germany, Denmark, and Sweden—their faces covered with grizzly beards, and their teeth clenched upon a pipe stem. . . . Neither cold nor storm stopped them in their journey to the promised land, on the frontiers of which they had now arrived."

Factories that made farming tools sprouted in Chicago. So did blacksmith, wagon, and coachmaker's shops. When railroads were laid out in the 1840s, the flat land around Chicago helped make the city a major rail center.

SECTION 3 REVIEW

1. Name three ways in which farming in the Northwest differed from farming in the South.
2. In what ways was the Northwest well suited for farming with machines?
3. What kinds of goods were made in Cincinnati? In Chicago?
4. Out of every 100 people in the Northwest in 1850, how many lived in cities?

Reading Skills

It helps to know the difference between <u>general</u> and <u>specific</u>. For example, "people" is a general term (includes many) while "the boys" is specific (includes a few). In each pair below, which is general?

1. machines/reapers
2. shovel/tool
3. crop/wheat

CHAPTER 16 ACTIVITIES

Wordpower!

Match the letter of each term with the number of its definition.

a. sectionalism   d. overseer
b. tenement   e. reaper
c. dormitory

1. building in which many people share rooms
2. person who supervised the work of slaves
3. machine for harvesting grain
4. building divided into many small apartments
5. loyalty to one part of the country

Reading Skills

Review the chapter introduction to choose the best ending for each sentence below.

1. The main subject is:
   a. industry   b. farming   c. parts of America
2. The information about Davis and Lincoln:
   a. illustrates the subject
   b. is part of the subject
   c. is not part of the subject
3. An overview of each section appears at:
   a. the beginning   b. the middle   c. the end

Writing Skills

Imagine that you lived and worked in one section of the country in 1815–1850. Each night you write in a diary, keeping a record of the changes in your life and your growing pride in the section. Write three or four imaginary diary entries of about 50 words each.

Figure It Out

Between 1815 and 1850, the need for lighting in factories and homes caused a demand for whale oil, which was used in lamps. Many New England fishermen turned to whaling. American ships sailed to all parts of the globe to catch whales. Study the world map at the back of the book to answer the questions.

1. The whaling grounds nearest to Massachusetts lay between Greenland and Canada. Describe the route ships would follow to reach these grounds.
2. Describe the route going from Massachusetts to New Zealand and back.
3. The page from a log book shows how sailors killed the whales, removed their oil, and left the dead bodies to rot in the ocean. If a whale yielded 80 barrels of oil and the ship could hold 1,500 barrels, how many whales could sailors kill before returning home?

A page from a whaler's log book

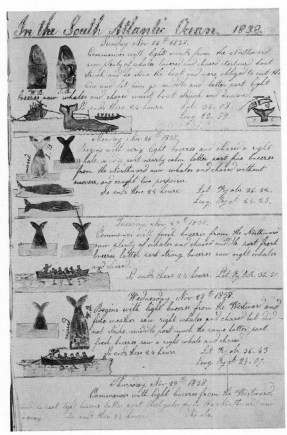

CHAPTER 17

Ties of National Unity

On July 4, 1826, exactly 50 years after the signing of the Declaration of Independence, Thomas Jefferson died at his home in Virginia and John Adams died in Massachusetts. The two men had been close friends when they worked together on the Declaration 50 years earlier. It seemed to many Americans that their deaths on such an important date were a sign from God to remind Americans of their past.

Memories of the past helped strengthen **nationalism**—a feeling that Americans belonged together in a separate country. The last chapter discussed changes from 1815 to 1850 that led to sectionalism. This chapter considers changes that united Americans. Section 1 is about transportation and communication. Section 2 is about trade and business.

Glossary terms

nationalism
subsistence
internal improvements
turnpike
navigable waterway

SECTION 1 Travel and Communication

Until about 1815, most Americans farmed for **subsistence** only. That is, farm families produced enough from garden, field, and woods to feed, clothe, and house themselves. They had little reason to increase the size of their crops, because they had no good way to get crops to market.

Internal Improvements

In the early 1800s, national leaders began calling for a program of improved transportation or **internal improvements.** Turnpikes, steamboats, canals, and railroads all improved transportation and led to changes in people's ways of living.

Roads. In 1815, most roads in the United States were between poor and pathetic. Many were little more than broad paths cut through the woods. In wet places, they offered a line of ruts and mud holes, in dry places, a deep layer of dust. No wonder that **turnpikes**, leveled and topped with crushed stone, became popular between 1810 and 1830. Best known was the Cumberland or National Road, which cut across the eastern United States (see map on next page).

Private companies built many other turnpikes, mostly in the North. By collecting tolls, they hoped to get back what they spent on road building. Unfortunately, most didn't

Reading Skills

For each of the following ordinary words, which meaning is the best in the context of the paragraph labeled "Roads"?
1. Pathetic (line 2)
   a. poor quality
   b. something to feel sorry for
2. Cut (line 7)
   a. slice   b. make a path

Freight Rates*

	1816	1853
Turnpikes	$30.00 and up	$15.00
Mississippi or Ohio River, shipping downstream	1.30	.37
Mississippi or Ohio River, shipping upstream	5.80	.37
Erie Canal	not built	1.10
Ohio Canal	not built	1.10
Erie Railroad	not built	2.40

*Average rates to move 1 ton of goods 1 mile.

This map shows important roads about 1840, including the Cumberland, or National Road. Begun in Cumberland, Maryland, in 1811, it later reached central Illinois. Parts of it remain today near U.S. Highway 40 and Interstate 70. What states did the National Road pass through? Why do you think there were no roads west of the Mississippi River?

**Major Roads
About 1840**

▭ Roads

0   200   400 MILES
0 200   400 KILOMETERS

56

make much money. Carrying goods by wagon, even on a good road, was slow and expensive.

Waterways. What could not easily be pulled by wagon could be carried by water. Knowing this, early settlers had settled near **navigable waterways**—rivers or bodies of water deep enough for ships.

The big problem with river travel was finding a way to move upstream against the current. Some farmers floated their crops downstream on rafts. When they reached the market, they sold the boat or raft as lumber and walked home.

Robert Livingston and Robert Fulton offered an answer to traveling upstream with their steamboat, *Clermont*. Powered by a steam engine, it made its first successful run in 1807. Nowhere did steamboats become more important for carrying goods and people than on the Mississippi. By 1855 there were 727 steamboats on the river.

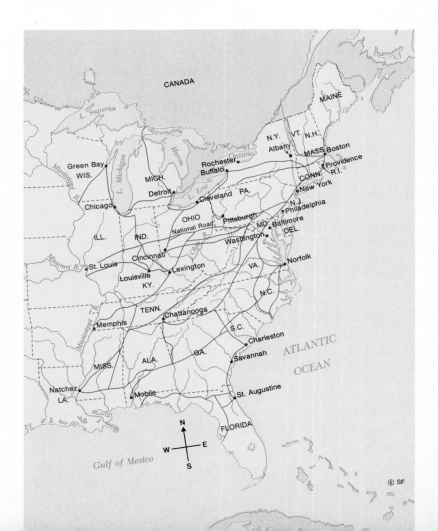

The steamboat was not the only response to poor travel by water. A second answer was the canal. Between 1815 and 1840, more than 3,000 miles of canal were dug in the United States. As the map below shows, canals connected rivers and cities. Most famous was the Erie Canal, which crossed 364 miles from Albany in eastern New York State to Buffalo in the west. When completed in 1823, it brought a dramatic drop in the cost of shipping. This drop and others are shown in the table on the facing page.

Railroads. The most important form of transportation in the 1800s was the railroad. Railroads began to be built in the 1830s. Their greatest growth came *after* 1850. Yet even by 1850, they had become a major way to carry people and goods. Horses pulled the first trains, but steam engines soon replaced them. With improvements, travel by rail became the fastest way to move.

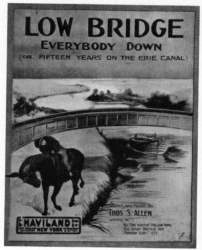

Mules towed canal boats. When a boat went under a bridge, everyone on board had to duck.

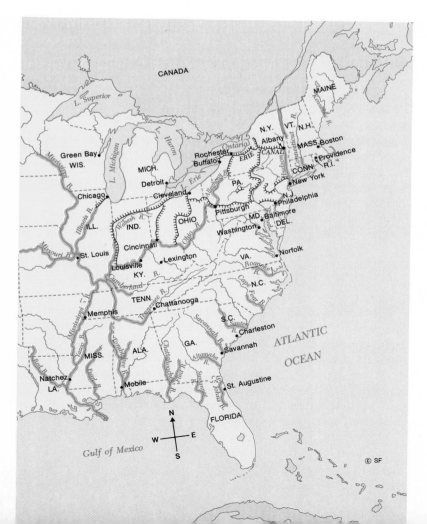

This map shows navigable waterways—those that could be traveled by large boats—about 1840. Name six of these waterways.

Navigable Waterways About 1840

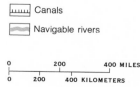

| | Canals |
| | Navigable rivers |

0 · 200 · 400 MILES
0 · 200 · 400 KILOMETERS

Improving Communications

You may remember reading that the War of 1812 ended six weeks before anyone in the United States knew about it. There were no fast ways to send messages. Mails were only as fast as the different forms of transportation.

Samuel F. B. Morse, a Massachusetts artist, invented a machine—the telegraph—that greatly helped communications. It carried messages over wires in code. On May 24, 1844, Morse showed that the telegraph could work by sending a message from Washington to Baltimore, 40 miles away. Within a few years telegraph wires had been strung to New York City, Chicago, New Orleans, and other large cities.

Using a telegraph, a person could receive a message a second after it was sent. Railroad companies used the telegraph to make train service safer and more regular. Newspapers also found the telegraph useful. Only weeks after Morse's demonstration, a reporter sent a news story by telegraph. Up until this time, newspaper owners gathered out-of-town news by mail. As soon as papers could get stories by wire, people all over the country could be reading and thinking about the same events right after they had taken place.

SECTION 1 REVIEW

1. Name four important ways of carrying people and goods between 1815 and 1850.

2. In what years did each of the following take place: (a) the first steamboat trip, (b) start of the National Road, (c) completion of the Erie Canal, (d) the first railroads built?

3. In 1853, how much did it cost to carry two tons of boards 100 miles by (a) turnpike wagon, (b) Mississippi River steamboat, (c) Erie Canal boat?

4. Name two ways the telegraph helped tie Americans together.

Glossary terms

economy	**panic**
capital	**depression**
corporation	**recovery**
dividend	**prosperity**

SECTION 2 Ties of Trade and Business

Between 1815 and 1850, Americans began to depend on one another more and more. Factory owners depended upon farmers and planters to buy their goods, while farmers and planters depended upon people in cities and factory towns to buy their crops. America was turning from a subsistence economy to a cash **economy.** Instead of making everything they needed, more and more families produced goods or crops that they sold for cash. They then used the cash to buy

goods or crops they needed. Changes in business made possible this change from one kind of economy to another. And, as always happens, these changes led to still others.

New Ways in Business

Capital is money put to a productive use—to build roads, railroads, farms, plantations, and businesses. Americans got capital in different ways. Capital for roads, canals, and railroads often came from governments. Much of the capital for the first factories came from people who had made money in trade. Capital to buy land and build farms and plantations came from the savings of farmers and planters themselves. Europeans also put up a great deal of capital.

Between 1815 and 1850, Americans felt a need to make it easier to raise capital because they were setting up businesses that required a great deal of money to get started. As a result, they made it easier to form a **corporation.** A corporation is a group of persons given the power to carry on a business. A corporation puts together money to start a business by selling stock. The stock is sold in units called shares. Each share of stock represents a share in the ownership of the business. The shares can be bought by people who wish to own part of a company. They can be sold if a person no longer wishes to own part of a company. The stockholders own the company. If the company makes money, they receive **dividends.** If the company loses money, the price of its stock goes down. Starting in 1837, the states passed laws making it easier for a company to become a corporation.

Americans began depending on one another for goods and services. A farm family might bring its apples to a cider press (top) and pay to have them made into cider. In cities, boot cleaners (bottom) went from house to house collecting work.

59

Peddlers sold goods from the back of a wagon (top). In a city, a butcher might set up a stall on the street and cut meat for buyers (bottom).

Changes in Trade

At one time, foreign trade had been divided among many seaports on the Atlantic coast. After 1815, the larger ports grew bigger and busier than ever while the smaller ones lost business. This happened because of changes in transportation. There was no point in using a port if it did not have roads, canals, or rails nearby to carry goods elsewhere.

Boston, Philadelphia, Baltimore, New York, and New Orleans became the leading ocean ports. Most imports came to New York and went by wagon, boat, or railroad to places throughout America. In the export trade, New Orleans led. It shipped the southern crops that made up two thirds of all American exports.

The United States traded with most of the nations of the world but did most of its business with England. Steam-powered ships began operating between New York City and England in 1819. They carried people, light freight, and mail. By 1850, the crossing time was only about ten days.

Trade within the United States grew more quickly than foreign trade. With better transportation, farmers, planters, and manufacturers could reach wider markets than before.

Ways of getting goods differed. In cities and larger towns, stores began to specialize in groceries, dry goods, hardware, or other goods. In villages and smaller towns, general stores sold everything. But many people depended upon wandering peddlers to sell them such goods as pins, combs, and clocks.

The American System

With the changes in the economy between 1815 and 1850, no one section of the country had everything it needed. To get what they needed and sell what they made, the three sections had to trade with one another and with other nations.

Senator Henry Clay called this the "American system." He wanted the United States to grow in such a way that the differences between sections strengthened the whole country. He thought business needs would tie Americans together.

On paper, the "American system" seemed to run smoothly. In the real world, it did not. The differences in business interests led to conflict. As factories grew in the Northeast and Northwest, factory owners asked Congress to pass high tariffs to protect their businesses. Southerners, however, depended upon exports. They wanted low tariffs and free trade. In 1832, South Carolina threatened to leave the Union unless Congress repealed the high tariffs.

The Modern Business Cycle

A cash economy also presented new problems. For everything that Americans gained, they lost something as well. For example, although people could make more money working for a factory instead of on a farm, they now had to depend on factory owners for jobs. However, factory owners also had to depend on others. Although they could make more money with a big factory than with a small shop, they had to find many more customers. They also had to persuade bankers and investors to loan them money to carry on business.

Many people became connected to one another by loans and investments. If one person failed to pay a debt on time, others would be unable to pay their debts. Businesses could fail if too many customers could not pay what they owed. During the 1800s, business failures changed. They spread rapidly from one part of the nation to another, from Europe to the United States, and from the United States to Europe. They also arrived so regularly that historians say they were part of the modern business cycle.

The business cycle had four stages: panic, depression, recovery, and prosperity. A **panic** started with people rushing to the banks to get their money out. Many banks closed down, and businesses could no longer get loans or investments. As a result, many factories cut production or went out of business. This meant workers lost their jobs and could not buy as much as they wanted. In the hope of selling their crops, many farmers and planters lowered their prices. However, they then found themselves unable to pay their debts, and they lost their land. Soon the country was in the depths of a **depression**. After three or four years, **recovery** began. Those people who still had jobs or money began investing. Eventually the country enjoyed **prosperity** once more. During the 1800s, a panic leading to a depression took place about every twenty years—the first in 1819.

SECTION 2 REVIEW

1. What is a corporation? Why did Americans make it easier to form corporations in the 1800s?
2. How did trade tie Americans together?
3. What happened to small seaports from 1815 to 1850? Why?
4. Name three ways in which Americans came to depend more on one another in this period.
5. What are the four stages of the modern business cycle?

The four stages of the modern business cycle

The Business Cycle

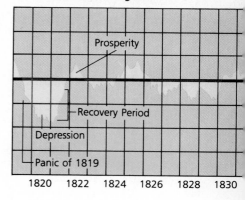

Prosperity

Recovery Period

Depression

Panic of 1819

1820   1822   1824   1826   1828   1830

Reading Skills

The fifth paragraph on page 60 explains the different ways that goods got to customers. Which list of ways below is given in the same order as the text?

1. a. specialty stores
   b. general stores
   c. peddlers
2. a. grocery stores
   b. hardware stores
   c. peddlers

CHAPTER 17 ACTIVITIES

Wordpower!

Write clues for the terms in the crossword puzzle.

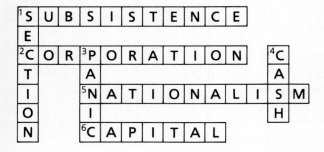

Across

1.
2.
5.
6.

Down

1.
3.
4.

Reading Skills

Examine the following pairs to decide which item in each pair is the <u>cause</u> and which is the <u>effect</u>.

1. Mills had to be within a half-day wagon trip for farmers and were therefore small.
   a. Mills had to be within a half-day wagon trip.
   b. Mills were small.
2. People who wished to raise a great deal of capital for a business formed a corporation.
   a. People formed a corporation.
   b. People wished to raise capital.
3. If people took all their money out of banks, businesses could not get capital.
   a. People took money out of banks.
   b. Businesses could not get capital.

Writing Skills

Despite the strong sectional feelings between 1815 and 1850, a number of changes during those years pulled the country together. Write a one-paragraph essay pointing out two or three of those changes and explaining how each one helped unite the country.

Figure It Out

Messages went over telegraph wires in the code that Samuel Morse invented. The sender clicked out a message on the machine. A short click was called a "dot" (.), and a longer click was called a "short dash" (—) or a "long dash" (——). Pauses between clicks told the telegraph operator where letters or words ended.

Using the Morse Code, figure out the message below. A slash (/) shows where a letter ends, and a double slash (//) shows where a word ends.

Morse Code

CHAPTER 18

People and Prejudice

In studying history you will often find that a **minority** group is the victim of **prejudice**. During the early 1800s, three groups in America often faced prejudice. Black people, Indians, and immigrants were mistreated in all parts of the country. However, each group faced the most prejudice in the section in which it was the largest minority. This chapter considers how these minority groups were treated. Section 1 is about Indian removal. Section 2 is about immigrants. Section 3 is about slavery.

SECTION 1 Indian Removal

Until 1803, government leaders believed that given enough time, Indians would become "civilized" Christian farmers. After buying the Louisiana Territory in 1803, President Jefferson had a new idea. Since it was taking the Indians a long time to become like whites, why not encourage tribes to move out of the "second West" into the land beyond the Mississippi?

After the War of 1812, the United States government made treaties with the Indians to buy their lands and get them to move west. Leading this effort was General Andrew Jackson. Right behind him was a hungry bunch of land speculators.

An 1817 treaty with the Cherokees offers an example of how Jackson operated. He told Cherokee leaders that an agreement they had once made with President Jefferson bound them to sell their eastern lands. When the Cherokee council denied this, Jackson made each member stand up and say whether he wanted to call Jefferson a liar. The Cherokees were too respectful to do this, and so Jackson got their land. In fact, Jefferson had never made such an agreement with the Cherokee.

Using bribery and fear, Jackson worked out eight other treaties between 1814 and 1824. The Indians gave up one-fifth of Georgia and Mississippi, one-third of Tennessee, and three-quarters of Alabama and Florida. This land was opened to white settlement. The Indians remained on their shrunken lands, hoping to stay.

Glossary terms

minority
prejudice
defraud

Reading Skills

Locating and recognizing para-graph topics requires skill. Re-read the fourth paragraph on this page to choose the best endings below.

1. The best statement of the para-graph's topic is:
   a. the 1817 treaty with the Cherokees
   b. how Jackson got land from the Cherokees
2. The topic sentence of this para-graph is located:
   a. at the beginning   b. at the end

SEQUOYAH
(1770?–1843)

As a child growing up in the Cherokee town of Taskigi, in what is now Tennessee, Sequoyah lived as any other Cherokee boy. He hunted in the deep forests of his homeland. He spoke not a word of English and rarely saw white people.

All that was to change after Sequoyah was hurt while hunting. Unable to hunt, Sequoyah became a silversmith. He made such beautiful jewelry that it was sought after by his people and white traders alike.

Sequoyah came to know white ways well and became very interested in the power of their "talking leaves"—books. No tribe in what is now the United States had a written language of its own. Sequoyah believed that if the Cherokee were to preserve their ways of life and compete with whites, they would have to have a written language. In 1809 he began inventing a Cherokee alphabet, not an easy job. After 12 years' work, he took the secret of writing to all the Cherokee people. Soon newspapers and books were printed in their language.

Sequoyah became the most famous Indian of his time. He visited Washington and met the President in 1828. People from all over the country came to visit him.

In 1829, Jackson became President. Congress soon passed the Indian Removal Act (1830), which gave the President power to try to convince the Indians to leave. The law was hotly debated in Congress, and the vote was close. Many northeasterners were against the shoddy way westerners and the government were treating the Indians. However, Jackson got his way.

The Removals

Surrendering to pressure, the Indians moved. For example, in November, 1831, about 4,000 Choctaw set out. A French writer who happened to be present wrote:

> At the end of the year 1831, while I was on the left bank of the Mississippi, at a place named . . . Memphis, there arrived a numerous band of Choctaws. . . . It was then the middle of winter, and the cold was unusually severe; the snow had frozen hard upon the ground, and the river was drifting huge masses of ice. The Indians had their families with them, and they brought in their train the wounded and the sick, with children newly born and old men on the verge of death. They possessed neither tents nor wagons, but only their arms and some provisions. ""

Large numbers of the Choctaw died in the move west. Their experience was soon repeated by the Creek and the Cherokee.

In 1832, the Creeks signed a treaty that gave them five years to sell their property and get ready for the trip west. The next four years saw one of the worst scandals in American history. Speculators **defrauded** the Creeks of most of their property. Since state laws prevented an Indian from testifying against a white man, the courts supported any claim by a white to have bought land from an Indian. As one speculator put it, "Hurrah, boys—here goes it—let's steal all we can."

When fraud charges reached Jackson's ears, he ignored them. The official in charge of Indian affairs excused the speculators by saying: "Our citizens were disposed to buy and the Indians to sell." If the Indians wasted their land, "it is deeply to be regretted." Driven to the forests and begging for food, some Creeks refused to move by the 1837 deadline. This Jackson did not ignore. He ordered them to be rounded up, put in chains, and sent west with the rest of their people.

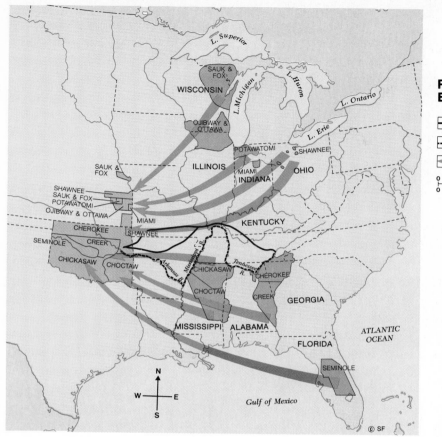

Removal of the Eastern Indians

▭ Cherokee Trail of Tears land route
▭ Cherokee Trail of Tears water route
◅ Other Indian removals

0   150   300 MILES
0   150   300 KILOMETERS

In 1838 and 1839, though Jackson was no longer President, his policies continued. The Cherokees were forced west. They left their homes in North Carolina, Tennessee, and Georgia for what would one day be called Oklahoma. Like the Choctaw and Creek, they were moved by "contractors" hired by the government. A typical contractor was paid $20 an Indian. To make money, contractors fed the Indians rotten meat, clothed them in rags, and carried them across rivers on unsafe boats. One quarter of the Cherokees died, and the survivors called their move the "Trail of Tears."

Indian removal was, of course, carried out with further promises. The map above shows the new land Indians were given. In the words of President Andrew Jackson, this new land west of the Mississippi was to be theirs, "as long as grass grows or water runs."

This map shows the removal of the Eastern Indians. What states were the original homes of the Shawnee? Sauk and Fox? Potawatomi? Ojibway and Ottawa? Cherokee? Creek? Chickasaw? Miami? Choctaw? Seminole?

The Cherokee Trail of Tears

SECTION 1 **REVIEW**

1. Why did Jefferson suggest moving Indians west?
2. How did Jackson get Indians to move?
3. What evidence is there in the section that some white Americans disapproved of Indian removal?
4. Given his treatment of the Indians, do you think Jackson deserves to be called a great President? Explain.

Glossary terms

native
nativist

SECTION 2 **Immigrants in the North**

Between 1815 and 1860, more than 5 million persons came to the United States. The main reason was economic. Immigrants hoped to make a better living in America than they had at home. As the largest minority in the North, immigrants faced special problems.

The Irish were the first to arrive in huge numbers during the 1800s. They came because their main food crop—potatoes—failed. When a disease destroyed the crop for four years in a row (1843–1847), half a million Irish starved to death. A million others fled to the United States. They made up the largest group of immigrants between 1815 and 1860. Most settled in cities in the Northeast. Few went inland to look for farms because they had no money to buy land or, for that matter, even a railroad ticket.

Germans made up the second largest group of foreign-born in the United States. Most were peasants or farmers. Many came for political reasons. They were not as poor as the Irish, and many brought enough money to buy farms. Still, many Germans chose to remain in eastern cities.

Opposition to Immigrants

A person born in a country is a **native.** Someone who thinks natives are better than immigrants is called a **nativist.** In the 1840s and 1850s, American nativists worried about growing immigration. They believed that the newcomers would increase poverty and crime and take over the American government.

About half the German immigrants and nearly all the Irish were Catholics. Because most Americans were Protestant, they distrusted Catholics. Anti-Catholic writers said the immigrants were part of a plot to put the Pope in control of America. Nativists often refused to hire Catholics, especially Irish Catholics. "No Irish need apply" was a common ending for job ads. In the 1840s, anti-Catholic riots broke out in many cities.

A number of nativist groups formed. In 1854, they began a political party—the Native American, or American, party. Outsiders called it the Know-Nothing party because the members said "I know nothing" whenever they were asked about the party's secrets. The party's "America for Americans" slogan drew many voters.

Immigrants at Work

For immigrants in the 1830s, life in the United States was somewhat better than for those in the 1840s or 1850s. The later immigrants faced greater prejudice, in part because so many more of them came.

Men commonly sought work digging canals, building railroads, laying streets, or doing other hard labor. Women worked in cotton mills or took jobs as servants, laundresses, or seamstresses. Children were especially wanted for work in the mills, because they were small enough to work in back of

National Origin of Immigrants 1820–1860

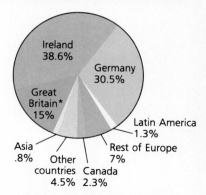

Ireland 38.6%
Germany 30.5%
Great Britain* 15%
Latin America 1.3%
Asia .8%
Rest of Europe 7%
Other countries 4.5%
Canada 2.3%

*Great Britain included England, Scotland, Wales, and Northern Ireland.
Total number of immigrants: 5,062,414

Reading Skills

Study the circle graph above to choose the correct ending below:
1. The graph represents:
   a. one state
   b. one region
   c. one period of time
2. The numbers in the graph represent:
   a. number of American-born and foreign-born people
   b. percent of foreign-born people
   c. percent of American-born people

This sketch shows an immigrant family working in a cotton spinning mill. Note the small child behind the threads (lower left). Because immigrants were willing to work for lower pay, they replaced native American workers in many mills.

certain machinery. Many children also worked at sewing or sold newspapers.

Besides refusing to hire immigrants, many nativists took advantage of them, paying them less than they would native Americans. The willingness of immigrants to accept low pay frightened some natives. They were afraid they would lose their jobs to immigrants who were willing to accept lower pay. However, immigrants competed with each other for jobs as well as with earlier settlers. They also competed with free blacks for jobs. An Englishman who visited New York in 1843 wrote:

"It is a curious fact that the poorer class of Irish immigrants in America are more in favor of continuing slavery than any portion of the population in the free states. I tried to discover the cause of this strange situation and learned that ten or twelve years ago, the lowest jobs, such as porters, dock-laborers, waiters at hotels, stable boys, boot-cleaners, barbers, were all, or nearly all, black men. Nearly all the maid servants, cooks, washerwomen, were black women. They used to get very good wages for these jobs. But within the last few years there has been a great [increase] of unskilled laborers from Ireland, England, and other countries, into New York, Boston, Philadelphia, and other large towns in the eastern states. These immigrants press into these low jobs (because they can find no other), offering to labor for any wages they can get. They have reduced the wages of the blacks and deprived great numbers of them of employment. Hence, there is a deadly hatred between them, and quarrels and fights among them occur daily. . . . The white people reason thus: Competition among free white working men here is even now reducing our wages daily. If the blacks were to be freed, probably hundreds of thousands of them would move into these northern states. The competition for employment would increase so much that wages would very speedily be as low, or lower here, than they are in Europe. Better, therefore, for us, that [blacks] remain slaves as they are."

SECTION 2 REVIEW

1. What was the main reason immigrants came to the United States?
2. Give two reasons that nativists opposed immigrants.
3. Why did many immigrants favor slavery?

SECTION 3 Slavery

How slaves lived and worked has long been controversial. Historians do not agree on what slave conditions were like in the 1800s. What follows are statistics and short summaries, each giving a general picture of slavery in the mid-1800s. The summaries take different historians' views into account.

Black Americans 1790–1860

| | North | | South | |
	Free	Slave	Free	Slave
1790	27,034	40,086	32,523	657,538
1800	47,196	36,505	61,239	857,097
1810	78,181	27,510	108,265	1,163,852
1820	99,307	19,108	134,327	1,518,914
1830	137,529	3,568	182,070	2,005,475
1840	170,728	1,129	215,565	2,486,226
1850	196,308	262	238,187	3,204,051
1860	226,152	64	261,918	3,953,696

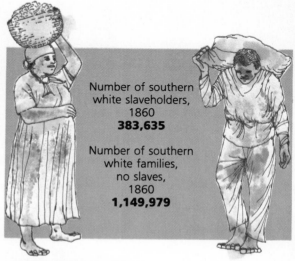

Number of southern white slaveholders, 1860
383,635

Number of southern white families, no slaves, 1860
1,149,979

Southern White Slaveholders 1860

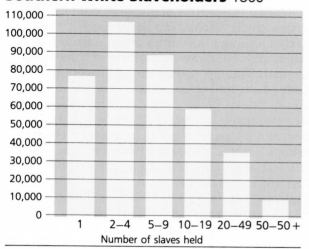

Number of slaves held: 1, 2–4, 5–9, 10–19, 20–49, 50–50+

What Slaves Ate

Food	Calories per day	% of energy from each food
Corn	2,803	66.6
Pork	685	16.3
Sweet Potatoes	233	5.5
Cowpeas	149	3.5
Wheat	138	3.3
Beef	96	2.3
Butter/Milk	88	2.1
White Potatoes	14	.4
Total	4,206	100

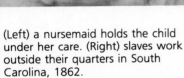
(Left) a nursemaid holds the child under her care. (Right) slaves work outside their quarters in South Carolina, 1862.

Diet and nutrition. Corn was the most important food for slaves, with pork a rather weak second. One estimate of food per day is shown in the table on page 69. This was enough to give slaves energy to work, but it was a boring diet.

Shelter. The slave family lived in a one-room log, board, or brick cabin less than 20 feet square. One estimate is that 15 feet square was typical. In this space lived an average of five to six persons. Although probably better than slums for some white workers in the North, these were worse than the housing for most free Americans. Some cabins were carefully built and whitewashed inside, but many were crudely built, drafty, and dirty, with clay floors and leaky roofs.

Clothing. Yearly clothing allowances differed from place to place. Two or three pairs of pants and shorts may have been the average. Kenneth Stampp, a well-known historian, has written that most adults and children went without shoes even in winter and did not have enough clothing to keep warm in freezing weather.

Kinds of labor. Not all slaves were field workers. On large plantations perhaps half the slaves did not do regular field work. They included small children, old slaves, cripples, and, sometimes, pregnant slaves or nursing mothers. These slaves were labeled "quarter hands," "half hands," or "three-quarter hands" and were given lighter work, such as spinning or cleaning the grounds. Many favored slaves worked as servants. Slaves with special skills worked full time as carpenters, coopers, masons, and millers. Also, almost a half million slaves lived in towns and cities. They worked as servants, railroad builders, drivers, miners, deck hands, and in hundreds of other jobs.

Working hours. The slave working day depended upon the season, the type of work, and the place. Some slaves on cotton plantations along the coast had an early afternoon quitting time. Some slaveholders, especially in Virginia's tired tobacco fields, did not push their slaves hard. However, many southern slaves worked from "day clean to first dark" during the growing season. Whether slaves worked longer hours than northern factory workers no one can be sure. What is certain is that if slaves did not like the hours, they could not quit.

Slave sales and family stability. Historians do not agree about how often slave sales broke up families. Sales forceably ended between 10 and 30 percent of slave marriages. Also, children were sometimes sold away from their parents. However, some owners tried not to break up families, or they sold only to neighbors. Still, every slave family knew that, at any time, a member of the family could be sold off.

Punishment and resistance. Historians do not agree on how severely slaves were treated. Whipping was common in some places and ads for runaways often described scars of punishment. On the other hand, some owners never beat their slaves. What is known is that whipping was legal and did not surprise anyone when it happened. Slaves showed how they felt through a few full-scale revolts like the Nat Turner **insurrection** in Virginia in 1831. Still, little everyday protests like trashy cotton picking or leaving a gate open were more common. The depth of slave feeling is perhaps better seen in black folk songs like "Nobody Knows the Trouble I've Seen," and "All My Trials, Lord, Soon Be Over."

Laws. The Constitution did not give Congress power to pass laws about slavery. After 1808, the federal government could regulate the slave trade between states or with other countries. However, **states' rights** made regulating slavery or the slave trade within states the job of the state and local governments.

States and cities passed slave codes that described what slaves could not do. When times were tense, these codes were more strictly enforced. The table on the next page lists a sampling of these laws. The listed laws were not all in force at the same time and place.

FREDERICK DOUGLASS
(1817?–1895)

It is 1844. A tall, dignified black man is addressing a meeting of people opposed to slavery. In a deep and powerful voice, he tells of his days as a slave, how he escaped, how cruel the system is. The audience is deeply moved. After the meeting, someone says that he cannot believe that anyone who speaks so well could ever have been a slave. Slaves were born and lived in poverty and ignorance. The tall black man says that he will write a book to prove the truth of his story. That book was *Narrative of the Life of Frederick Douglass.*

Frederick Douglass was born a slave in Maryland. Although one master taught him to read and write, the beatings and neglect he suffered as a child were more typical. Even worse, he was not free.

After several tries, he escaped to Massachusetts. There, at a meeting of the American Anti-Slavery Society, he was asked to speak. His words were so powerful that from then on, he was famous. Douglass traveled in America, Europe, and Canada with his message: slavery is evil and it must be ended.

He spent the rest of his life working to free slaves and to win equal rights for black Americans.

71

Slave Laws

1. A child who had one slave parent and one free parent was free only if the free parent was his or her mother.

2. Slaves could not make any kind of contract, including marriage.

3. Slaves were not allowed to have weapons.

4. No one was allowed to teach slaves how to read or write. No one was allowed to give them books or pamphlets.

5. Slaves were not allowed to hit whites or insult them.

6. Any slave who went away from his or her plantation had to have a pass. The slave had to show this pass to any white who wanted to see it.

7. Slaves were not allowed to buy or possess liquor without the written consent of their owners.

8. Slaves were not allowed to own pigs, horses, or cattle or, in Mississippi, to grow their own cotton. They could, however, have their own gardens if the slaveholder let them.

9. Slaves could not conduct business without a permit or own any property.

10. Owners were required to feed and clothe their slaves properly and to take care of their sick and old slaves. If they failed to do so, they could be fined.

11. No slave could testify in court except in a case involving another slave.

12. It was illegal to mistreat or kill a slave unless the slave resisted punishment.

13. It was illegal for more than a few slaves (usually five) to gather together away from home unless a white was present.

14. It was illegal for a slaveholder to work slaves in the field on Sundays except as punishment or unless they were paid.

15. No slave was allowed to preach, except to the slaves on his or her home plantation in the presence of whites.

16. Most cities had laws controlling the behavior of slaves in public. For example, slaves in Charleston, South Carolina, were not allowed to swear, smoke, or walk with a cane.

Reading Skills

The best statement of the <u>overall purpose of this section</u> is:
1. to explain how slaves lived
2. to help you understand the tragedy of slavery in America
3. to show differences between northern and southern ways of life

SECTION 3 **REVIEW**

1. In 1860, how many free blacks were in the North? In the South?
2. How many white slaveholders had one slave? Two to four slaves? Five to nine slaves? Ten or more slaves?
3. "Three out of four white southern families owned at least one slave." What evidence supports or disagrees with this statement?
4. What kind of food, clothing, and housing did most slaves have?
5. Which slaves on large plantations were not expected to do a full share of work?
6. Consider 100 slave married couples. On the average, how many would have their marriages broken up by slave sales?
7. How did states' rights affect slave laws?
8. Why do you think laws forbade teaching slaves to read or write?

CHAPTER 18 ACTIVITIES

Wordpower!
Use each listed term in a sentence.
1. prejudice
2. minority
3. native
4. nativist
5. states' rights
6. insurrection

Figure It Out
Northern workers faced a hard life, whether they were native whites, free blacks, or immigrants. Study the two tables below and answer the questions.
1. Which workers made enough money to support a family of five?
2. How many family members would have to work to bring home a living wage as (a) cabinet-makers, (b) dressmakers, (c) teachers?
3. How does the cost of living in 1851 compare to what you would pay today?
4. What differences do you see in the necessities of life in 1851 and the necessities today?

Reading Skills
Examine the biographical sketches in this unit to decide the following:
1. The <u>subject</u> of each is:
   a. events   b. dates   c. a person
2. The <u>purpose</u> of each is:
   a. to tell events not in the regular text
   b. to show how specific people are part of history
   c. to explain a certain period of time

Writing Skills
To really understand someone else's thoughts and feelings, you have to put yourself in that person's shoes. Imagine that you were one of the following: an Indian, a new immigrant, or a black person, free or slave, between 1815 and 1850. One day a foreign visitor asks you how you feel about America. Write down what you might say in a couple of minutes to a visitor.

Cost of Living 1851*

Needs of a Family of Five	Cost per Week
Flour	$0.62½
Sugar (4 lbs.)	.32
Butter (2 lbs.), milk (2 cents per day)	.76½
Butcher's meat (2 lbs. beef per day)	1.40
Potatoes (½ bushel)	.50
Candlelight and fuel	.54
Furniture and utensils, wear and tear	.25
Rent	3.00
Clothing	2.00
Total	**$9.40**

*Minimum budget for a family of five. New York Daily *Tribune*, May 27, 1851.

Jobs and Wages 1840s and 1850s

Jobs	Weekly Wages	Hours Per Day
Cabinet-makers	$4.00–$6.00	12–14
Canal-horse drivers	2.00 – 3.00	12
Railroad workers	6.00	—
Dressmakers	1.25 – 1.75	14–16
Female mill workers	1.80 – 2.75 +	12
Fruit peddlers	3.00 – 5.00	—
Household servants	1.50 +	12
Machine makers	7.00 – 9.00	—
Teachers	1.00 – 4.00	—
Teamsters	5.00 – 7.00	12

+ Plus board

UNIT 6 TEST

In your notebook, write the answers to the following questions.

Completion

Fill in each blank with the term from the unit that best completes the sentence.

subsistence   segregated
spoils   rights
temperance   section
navigable

1. The _____ involves giving jobs to political workers.
2. Free blacks attended _____ schools separate from white students.
3. The _____ movement tried to end the making and selling of liquor.
4. A part of the country in which people have a great deal in common is a _____.
5. In 1815, most farmers grew enough for _____ but did not grow enough to sell.
6. _____ waterways are those that are deep enough for ships.
7. Under the Constitution, states' _____ let the states make laws about slavery.

Multiple Choice

Choose the ending that best completes each sentence.

1. The section of the country that produced special crops and made cotton cloth was:
   a. the Northeast
   b. the Northwest
   c. the South
2. The section of the country that grew tobacco and rice was:
   a. the Northeast
   b. the Northwest
   c. the South
3. The section of the country that produced large amounts of grain and meat was:
   a. the Northeast
   b. the Northwest
   c. the South
4. President James Monroe's eight years in office are called:
   a. the Age of Jackson
   b. the Era of Good Feelings
   c. the Era of Good and Bad Feelings
5. Until 1824, candidates for President were chosen only by:
   a. party conventions
   b. primary elections
   c. party caucuses
6. During the two terms of President Jackson:
   a. many more men could vote
   b. the spoils system took hold
   c. the eastern Indians lost most of their land
   d. all of the above
   e. none of the above
7. The first board of education appeared in:
   a. Mississippi
   b. Massachusetts
   c. New York
8. Most children's schooling in the early 1800s ended in:
   a. grade school
   b. secondary school
   c. college
9. The part of the country that was best suited for farming using machines was:
   a. the Northeast
   b. the Northwest
   c. the South
10. Waterfalls provided the power to run looms in this section of the country:
    a. the Northeast
    b. the Northwest
    c. the South

11. The weather was warm enough to grow cotton only in this section of the country:
    a. the Northeast
    b. the Northwest
    c. the South
12. An organization that can raise capital by selling stock is a:
    a. dormitory
    b. corporation
    c. share
13. People who think natives are better than immigrants are:
    a. nativists
    b. abolitionists
    c. sectionalists
14. The movement of the Cherokee from their homelands is called:
    a. the Oregon Trail
    b. the Trail of Tears
    c. the Cumberland Road
15. Slaves showed how they felt about not being free:
    a. through insurrections
    b. through purposely careless work
    c. through their songs
    d. through all of the above
    e. through none of the above

Finding Evidence

Copy each statement below. If the evidence in the text supports the statement, write "Supported" next to it. If the text challenges the statement, write "Challenged" next to it.
1. In 1860, most southern white families had slaves.
2. In 1850, most black Americans were slaves.
3. In 1850, most American women worked for wages.
4. By 1850, the South had as many big cities as the North.
5. President Jackson did nothing illegal in trying to move the eastern Indians to the West.
6. The Irish and the Germans were the largest immigrant groups between 1815 and 1850.

Reading Graphic Aids

Study the map to identify the listed places.
1. You are floating down the Ohio River. Indiana is on your right. What state is on your left?
2. This city is near the point where the Mississippi River empties into the Gulf of Mexico.
3. This state borders on four of the Great Lakes.
4. This state was famous for Lowell cotton mills.

Essay

Some historians have called the period from 1815 to 1850 a time of great progress. Write a paragraph agreeing or disagreeing with this statement. Include three facts from the unit.

A kitchen ball at White Sulphur Springs

THE PATH TO DISUNION

1840–1861

Between 1815 and 1850, two of the major forces at work in the United States were nationalism and sectionalism. Americans struggled to decide which was most important to them, the whole country or their particular part of the country.

In the 1840s and 1850s the struggle between these two forces was made worse by another force—the desire for the United States to grow. Many Americans wanted the United States to gain new lands belonging to Mexico and England. Others thought that adding new lands would simply bring more problems to American life by raising this question: What should be done with new lands? Many who were against adding land were reformers—people who wanted to make both people and society better. They feared that the United States would grow in such a way that slavery would spread.

The people who wanted America to grow had their way, and the United States reached the Pacific. But the price Americans paid was a terrible one. First, they fought a war with Mexico to gain a large chunk of the West. Then they argued among themselves to decide what should be done with the land, who should have the power to decide, and how the land should be governed.

At first, Americans found political compromises to answer these questions. As the 1850s drew to a close, however, politics stopped working, and Americans went to war with one another.

In this unit, you will see how American control spread across the whole continent. Then you will study the tragic results of a divided people.

TIME LINE

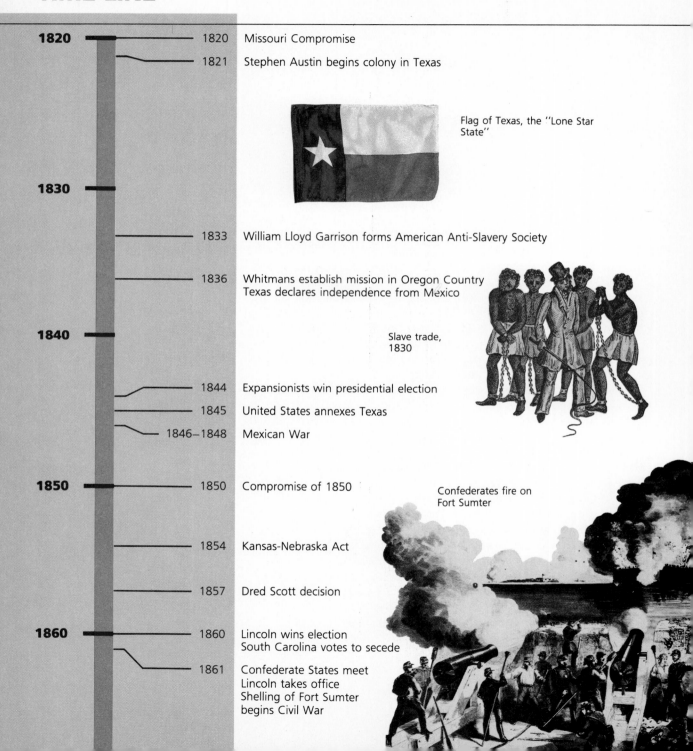

1820 — 1820	Missouri Compromise
— 1821	Stephen Austin begins colony in Texas

Flag of Texas, the "Lone Star State"

1830 —	
— 1833	William Lloyd Garrison forms American Anti-Slavery Society
— 1836	Whitmans establish mission in Oregon Country Texas declares independence from Mexico

Slave trade, 1830

1840 —	
— 1844	Expansionists win presidential election
— 1845	United States annexes Texas
— 1846–1848	Mexican War

1850 — 1850	Compromise of 1850

Confederates fire on Fort Sumter

— 1854	Kansas-Nebraska Act
— 1857	Dred Scott decision
1860 — 1860	Lincoln wins election South Carolina votes to secede
— 1861	Confederate States meet Lincoln takes office Shelling of Fort Sumter begins Civil War

CHAPTER 19

Manifest Destiny

In December, 1845, readers of the New York *Morning News* read these words by John L. O'Sullivan: "It is our **manifest destiny** to overspread and to possess the whole of the continent." He meant it was obviously God's will for Americans to move westward. Americans picked up his phrase "manifest destiny" and used it as the reason for moving west.

In this chapter, you will study where Manifest Destiny led Americans. In Section 1, you will read about the Oregon Country. In Section 2, you will study how Americans settled Texas. In Section 3, you will read about the Mexican War.

Glossary terms

manifest destiny
mountain men
missionary
emigrant

SECTION 1 The Oregon Country

People called **mountain men** broke the paths to the West. Most of them were beaver trappers who took off for the mountain streams for years on end and lived off the land. In the 1830s, families of settlers headed into the Oregon Country on the heels of the mountain men. The first were led by Marcus and Narcissa [när sis′ə] Whitman, Protestant **missionaries** who went to convert the Indians to Christianity and settled near what is now Walla Walla, Washington, in 1836.

Each year in the 1830s and 1840s, more and more Americans got "Oregon fever"—the urge to move to the Oregon Country. Thousands of **emigrants** left their homes to make their way by wagon train along the Oregon Trail to the Willamette [wi lam′ət] Valley. One traveler, Lucy Ann Henderson Deady, described the trip many years later.

“I was 11 years old when we crossed the plains in 1846, so my memories of the trip are very vivid. I remember how filled with terror I was by the violent thunderstorms along the Platte River. Our oxen would try to stampede, our tents would be blown down, and everybody and everything would be soaked with the driving rains. I remember with what terror I saw the Indians come out from Fort Laramie. The men got out their guns but all the Indians wanted was to see if we would give them anything.

Shortly after Narcissa Prentiss married Dr. Marcus Whitman in 1836, they set off for the Oregon Country. There they set up a mission to teach the Indians about Christianity. She taught school, and he cared for the sick.

We went south and then worked our way northward. While on our way to pass across the Cascade Mountains, we had to cross a desert that took two days' and one night's travel. There was no water at all, so we filled every keg and dish with water so that the cattle should have water as well as ourselves. We had no grain or hay for the cattle, so Mother baked up a lot of bread to feed them. When we had finally crossed the desert the cattle smelled water, and we couldn't stop them. They ran as hard as they could go, our

Find Lucy Deady's route on the map.

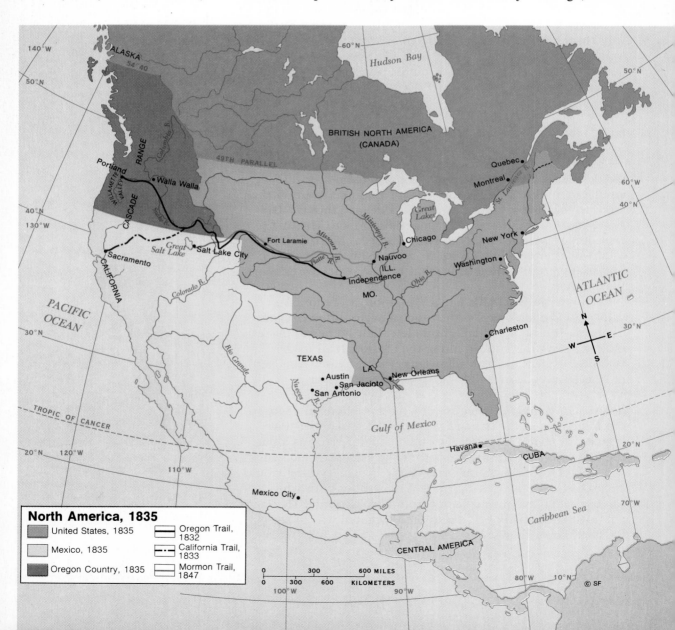

North America, 1835

▨ United States, 1835	▬ Oregon Trail, 1832
☐ Mexico, 1835	▬·▬ California Trail, 1833
▨ Oregon Country, 1835	▭ Mormon Trail, 1847

0   300   600 MILES
0   300   600   KILOMETERS

© SF

wagon bouncing along and nearly bouncing us out.

I shall never forget camp that night. Mother hung the bag containing the medicine from a nail on the sideboard of the wagon. My little sister got the bottle and drank it all. When Mother called her for supper she didn't come. Lettie had drunk the whole bottle of medicine. It was too late to save her life. We buried her there by the roadside in the desert.

Three days after my little sister Lettie died we stopped for a few hours and my sister Olive was born. We were so late that the men of the party decided we could not wait a day, so we had to press on. The going was terribly rough. We were the first party to take the Southern cutoff, so there was no road. The men walked beside the wagons and tried to ease the wheels down into the rough places, but in spite of this it was a very rough ride for my mother and her baby.

It was getting so late that at a meeting of the men of the wagon train it was decided to throw away every bit of surplus weight so that better speed could be made and so that the others should not have to wait for any overloaded wagons. A man named Smith had a wooden rolling pin that it was decided was useless and must be abandoned. I shall never forget how that big man stood there with tears streaming down his face as he said, "Do I have to throw this away? It was my mother's. I remember she always used it to roll out her biscuits, and they were awful good biscuits." He had to leave it, so they called him Rolling Pin Smith, a name he carried to the day of his death.

In coming north we followed the bed of a creek. It took us five days to make nine miles. I have never, before or since, seen such rough going. The cattle could hardly keep on their feet, and the wagons would occasionally tip over. We finally made our way northward, having very hard going as it was late in the year and the winter rains had started. We had been eight months on the road, instead of five, so we were out of food and our cattle were nearly worn out. We crossed the Willamette River by tying two canoes together and putting the wagons on them and ferrying them over. We stayed with an uncle who had settled south of Portland the year before, in 1845. We reached his cabin on December 17, 1846. **"**

Government

In the early 1800s, the Oregon Country had no government. Both the United States and England claimed the land. They agreed to let trappers from both countries work there.

Traveling west through Colorado

Reading Skills

Recognizing sequence, the order or arrangement of events and details, is a help in understanding history. On pages 79–81 are several paragraphs about the Oregon Trail from Lucy Ann Deady's story. Identify the correct sequence of the kinds of information Deady gives.
1. a. birth of Olive
   b. weather
   c. death of Lettie
2. a. weather
   b. death of Lettie
   c. birth of Olive
3. a. weather
   b. birth of Olive
   c. death of Lettie

As settlements grew, so did the need to agree about who owned the country. The more warlike of the Americans made their battle cry "54-40 or Fight." That meant they wanted the boundary between American and English claims to be at 54°40' north. The English, on the other hand, claimed land as far south as the Columbia River, near modern Portland. England had few settlers in this part of the country. The question of where to divide the Oregon Country became a key issue in the election of 1844. So did the ownership of Texas, which you will read about in the next section.

SECTION 1 REVIEW

1. What was Manifest Destiny?
2. How did mountain men help in the settlement of the West?
3. List four dangers emigrants faced on the Oregon Trail.
4. Who claimed to own the Oregon Country in the early 1800s?
5. What did "54-40 or Fight" mean?

SECTION 2 Texas

When Mexico won its independence from Spain in 1821, it claimed all of Spain's lands in the Southwest and West. Included were what are now Texas, Arizona, and New Mexico, which held several major Indian tribes and a few thousand whites. Also included was California, which had twenty-one Spanish religious **missions**, founded by Catholic priests, a few ports, and growing ranches.

Glossary terms

mission
annex

A detail from a painting of San Antonio, Texas, in the early 1800s shows *caballeros* (gentlemen), dressed in their holiday best, inviting the young lady of the house to a dance.

To encourage settlement, Mexico offered grants of land to anyone willing to move into sparsely settled places and become Mexican citizens and Catholics. In 1821, a Missouri man named Stephen Austin used such a grant to begin a colony of 300 American families in Texas. Good, cheap land was to be had there, and in the next 10 years, "Texas fever" brought thousands of Americans there.

As time passed, the Mexican government decided that letting Americans into Texas was a bad idea. First, the nearest Mexican government offices were 700 miles south of the Austin colony, too far away to enforce Mexican laws. Second, Americans and Mexicans disagreed about people's rights. Americans disliked being forced to join a particular church and doing without jury trials. Even after taking Mexican citizenship, many Americans did not feel loyal to Mexico.

Steps to War

Trouble came in 1827 and 1829 when Mexican laws tried to end slavery. Many Texans were outraged, for Texas held rich lands just right for cotton plantations. They became even more upset in 1830, when Mexico passed a law ending immigration by Americans and encouraging native Mexicans to settle in Texas.

A revolution in 1832 brought General Antonio Lopez de Santa Anna to power in Mexico. Texans asked Santa Anna to allow them to form a state government of their own and to have rights like those in the United States. Santa Anna's answer was to throw Stephen Austin, leader of the Texas colony, into jail for two years.

Texas rebels now had a reason to hold meetings, and meet they did. In response, Santa Anna forced the Texas provincial assembly to end its meeting. In 1835, he sent troops into Texas to take over the town cannons. The Texas rebels fought back. In October, 1835, Stephen Austin, newly freed from a Mexican jail, became commander of the Texas army.

War was on, and people from the United States signed up in Cincinnati, Louisville, and New Orleans to join the fight. After 187 Texans fought to the death against 3,000 Mexican soldiers at an old mission called the Alamo, the Texas battle cry became "Remember the Alamo!" In a major battle at San Jacinto in April, 1836, the Texans led by Sam Houston beat the Mexican army and took Santa Anna prisoner. They then forced him to sign a treaty recognizing the new Republic of Texas as an independent country.

SAM HOUSTON
(1793–1862)

Few Americans have lived more colorful lives than Sam Houston. He was governor of two states, congressman and senator from one, and twice president of a country other than the United States.

Born in Virginia, he grew up in Tennessee. As a teenager, he became interested in the Cherokee tribe and went to live with the Cherokees. They adopted him, giving him the name "Raven."

In the War of 1812, young Sam fought under Andrew Jackson and became his friend. After the war, Houston studied law. He became governor of Tennessee and then Congressman. Yet, problems with his marriage led him to leave the state to live with his Cherokee friends.

In 1833, Houston went to Texas. Always a strong leader, he led the American settlers in their war for independence from Mexico. They elected him the first president of the new republic.

After Texas became part of the United States, Houston became its senator. In 1860, he was elected governor. A backer of the Union, Houston retired before his term ended because the Texas legislature voted to leave the United States. Today a great city is named in his honor.

Reading Skills

Writers use quotation marks for different purposes. Re-read each use of quotation marks listed and decide whether the purpose of the quotation marks is to indicate: (a) a quoted statement made by someone not the author of the text, (b) a special use of a word or phrase, (c) a famous saying or slogan.

1. "Texas fever," (page 83, first paragraph)
2. "Remember the Alamo!" (same page, last paragraph)

Glossary terms

expansion
parallel

The Lone Star Republic

The Texans set up a government much like that of the United States, electing Sam Houston their first president. They then asked the United States to **annex** (take over) Texas and make it an American state. President Andrew Jackson refused. He feared a war with Mexico and believed that northerners would not allow another slave state into the Union.

Still hoping to be annexed, the Texans went about the business of running a separate country. They faced big problems. Their treasury was empty, their money had no gold or silver backing, and Mexico threatened to attack again.

SECTION 2 REVIEW

1. Why did Americans move into Texas?
2. How did Texas become an independent country?
3. Why did Andrew Jackson refuse to annex Texas?

SECTION 3 The Mexican War

In 1844, the United States faced a big question. Should it expand westward and bring more of North America under its control? Independent Texas still wanted to be annexed. The Oregon Country was becoming more American with every year. The Mexican state of California was a golden prize ready for the taking. Although most Americans believed in Manifest Destiny, many did not want to take over certain parts of North America. Northerners, in particular, did not want to add any new slave states.

The election of 1844 decided the question about **expansion**. James K. Polk, who favored growth, won. He then started work on a treaty with England about the Oregon Country. In 1846, he signed a treaty that set the United States boundary at the 49th **parallel**. Meanwhile, in December, 1845, Polk pushed Congress into annexing Texas as a state.

Steps to War

Ever since Texas had declared its independence, Mexico had warned the United States that annexing Texas would mean war. Nevertheless, Polk wanted to get still more land. He offered Mexico about $30 million for what are now California, New Mexico, and Arizona. Hurt by the loss of Texas and by American demands, the proud Mexicans refused. They also restated their claim to the land lying

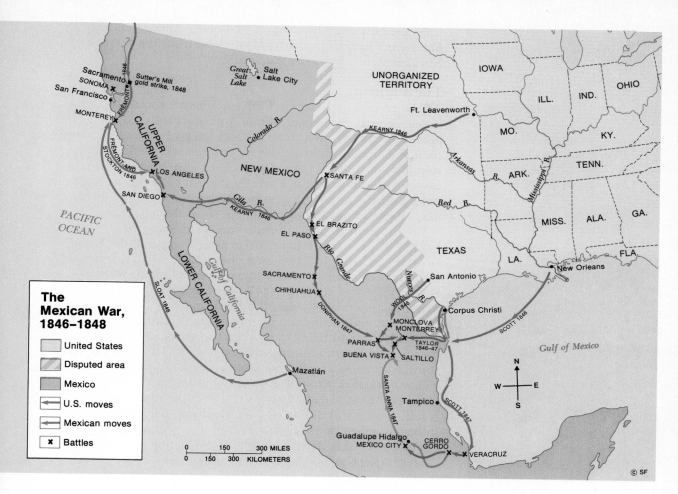

The Mexican War, 1846–1848

- United States
- Disputed area
- Mexico
- → U.S. moves
- → Mexican moves
- × Battles

0 150 300 MILES
0 150 300 KILOMETERS

© SF

between the Rio Grande and the Nueces [nwā'ses] River in Texas, land Americans also claimed. In January, 1846, Polk sent troops under General Zachary Taylor into this area.

Meanwhile, Polk had begun to work on California. In December, 1845, an American military man named John C. Frémont entered northern California with 60 mountain men. They were surveyors, but they were well armed for war. At the same time, Polk sent secret orders to a small fleet of United States ships to take California ports if war began.

The spark that touched off the war came on April 25, 1846, when Mexican troops attacked part of Zachary Taylor's army on the disputed land between the Rio Grande and the Nueces. At Polk's urging Congress declared war.

On the map above, trace the major actions of the Mexican War. First, locate the Nueces River, the Rio Grande, and the area between them claimed by both Mexico and the United States. Next, trace the campaigns of U.S. troops in Mexico in 1846 and 1847 under the following commanders: Zachary Taylor, John Wool, Alexander Doniphan, and Winfield Scott. Finally, trace the routes of John C. Frémont and Stephen W. Kearny in taking California. A U.S. fleet, first under John D. Sloat and then under Robert F. Stockton, supported this action.

To the battle cry of "Mexico or Death," thousands of Americans joined the army. Most came from the South and Northwest, few from the Northeast.

The Fighting

As soon as Americans in California heard about the declaration of war, they acted. While American ships captured the port of Monterey, American settlers led by Frémont declared their independence from Mexico and formed the Bear Flag Republic on July 5, 1846. Troops led by Stephen W. Kearny came overland from the East. By the fall of 1846, they had united all the American groups and captured all of California. They had also taken Santa Fe, New Mexico.

Yet the fighting in California was a sideshow. The main part of the war was fought in Texas and south of the Rio Grande. An army of 5,000 men under General Taylor moved into Mexico, where it met a Mexican army of 20,000 at Buena Vista in February, 1847. After tough fighting with many losses on both sides, the Mexican army retreated.

Polk wanted to find a way to end the fighting. He ordered General Winfield Scott to land on the Mexican coast and march over the mountains to Mexico City. This was the same route Hernando Cortés had taken some 300 years before.

Scott attacked Chapultepec [chə pul'tə pek], a rocky fortress that guarded Mexico City, in September, 1847. When it fell, the capital did as well. In the fight, teenage Mexican military cadets threw themselves off the cliff rather than be captured. To this day a statue of them stands in front of Chapultepec Castle. The war ended February 2, 1848.

Opposition to the War

Although many Americans thought the victories over Mexico were glorious, many others were against the war. They saw the war as a way to extend slavery. A famous poet said the war's backers wanted only "bigger pens to cram with slaves." A group called the American Peace Society grew.

One writer, Henry David Thoreau, showed how he felt by refusing to pay his taxes. He said that an evil government must be resisted in every way. He even said that if government is not just, people must break the law to keep from treating other people unjustly.

Another sharp critic of the war was a young Congressman from Illinois, Abraham Lincoln. In January, 1848, he delivered his famous "spot resolutions" in Congress, in which he

Scott's troops attack Chapultepec.

American soldiers shell Veracruz.

asked President Polk to name the spot where American blood had been shed on American soil by Mexicans. It took great courage for Lincoln to oppose the war. He came from a part of Illinois settled by southerners who wanted Texas. He lost the next election, partly because of his stand on the war.

Results

In the peace treaty signed at Guadalupe Hidalgo [gwä′dä-lü′pā ē däl′gō] in 1848, Mexico gave up almost half its territory, some 500,000 square miles. This included California and all the lands north of the Rio Grande. In return, America agreed to pay Mexico over $15 million.

Although the United States gained a great deal of land from the war, the cost was great. The question of whether to permit slavery in the new lands tore the United States apart. Nor would Mexico forget the way it lost its lands.

SECTION 3 REVIEW

1. What issue was decided by the election of 1844?
2. What were the underlying causes of the Mexican War? The immediate cause(s)? The spark?
3. What was the main reason that some Americans were against the Mexican War?
4. Thoreau would not pay his taxes because they went to support an evil government. What do you think he thought was evil about the government?

Reading Skills

Skim the section to identify the subject, purpose, and main idea.
1. The subject of this section is:
   a. war with Mexico
   b. Manifest Destiny
   c. California
2. The purpose is:
   a. to describe California
   b. to explain Manifest Destiny
   c. to show all sides of the Mexican War
3. The main idea is:
   a. America should not have taken California.
   b. America won a great victory.
   c. Even though the United States won the war, it lost much also.

CHAPTER 19 ACTIVITIES

Wordpower!
Match the letter of each term listed with the number of its definition.
a. Manifest Destiny   d. annex
b. emigrant   e. expansion
c. mission   f. parallel
  1. growth
  2. belief that fate guides American growth
  3. add land
  4. imaginary east-west line
  5. religious settlement
  6. person who moves within a country

Reading Skills
Which choice shows the relationship between Manifest Destiny and each Section title?
1. ''The Oregon Country''
  a. trappers   b. Oregon fever   c. Indians
2. ''Texas''
  a. Spain   b. slavery   c. Austin's colony

Writing Skills
Life in Oregon or Texas was dangerous. In a one-paragraph essay, explain three or four dangers people faced living in one of these areas in the 1840s.

Figure It Out
As Americans moved west, they often used meridians and parallels as boundary lines. Meridians and parallels are imaginary lines drawn on the globe.

In all, 360 meridian lines are drawn from the North Pole to the South Pole, dividing the earth into 360 equal parts. Each part is one degree (1°) of longitude. The Prime Meridian, which runs through England, is at 0° longitude. All other meridians are numbered east or west of the Prime Meridian. The 180° meridian, halfway around the earth from the Prime Meridian, is the greatest distance any point can be from the Prime Meridian.

Parallels are drawn from east to west. They measure distances north and south in degrees of latitude. The 0° parallel is the Equator. Parallels north and south of the Equator are numbered from 1° to 90°. The North Pole is at the 90th parallel north, the South Pole at the 90th parallel south.

Study the map and answer the questions.
1. At how many degrees of longitude is Greenwich? At about how many degrees of latitude?
2. What are the approximate latitudes and longitudes of the following places?
  a. New Orleans   c. Cairo   e. Dakar
  b. Pôrto Alegre   d. Maseru
3. Is South America east or west of the Prime Meridian?
4. Is the United States north or south of the Equator?

Longitude and Latitude

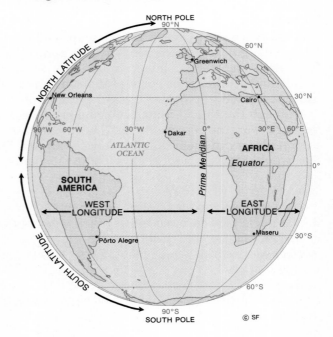

CHAPTER 20

The Slavery Question

Making decisions is a part of everyone's life and of every country's history, but it is not always easy. In fact, if it's easy to make a choice, there may not be much of a decision to make.

In making a decision, a person weighs the **alternatives**, or choices, tries to see the **consequences**, or results, of each action, and then chooses the way that seems best. Given the same choices, people with different ideas and beliefs may make different decisions.

After the war with Mexico, American leaders had to decide whether slaves would be allowed in the western lands. Abolitionists—people who wanted to end, or **abolish**, slavery—tried to keep slaves out of these new lands. In this chapter, you will study what American leaders decided and why. Section 1 is about abolitionism. Section 2 is about compromises over slavery.

Glossary terms

alternative   tactic
consequence   fanatic
abolish

SECTION 1 Abolitionism

Abolitionists were a small but important group of reformers from the 1820s to the 1850s. They worked hard to free the slaves and to end the slave trade.

Tactics

Like other reformers, the abolitionists used many tactics. A **tactic** is a way of acting that is planned to give a certain result. For example, a student who wants to meet a friend without appearing to do so may use the tactic of walking down a hall where he can "accidentally" meet the friend. Some tactics of the abolitionists worked well, and some did not.

In government. Abolitionists worked to get laws about slavery passed in the state governments and in Congress. Under the Constitution, Congress could not end slavery but could end the slave trade between states and with other countries. State governments could end both slavery and the slave trade within a state's boundaries.

In dealing with governments, the abolitionists used three main tactics. (1) They collected names on petitions that

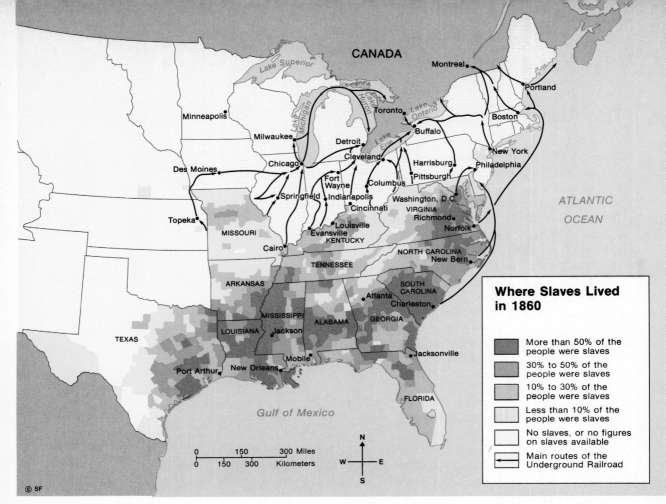

CANADA

Montreal

Portland

Lake Superior

Minneapolis

Toronto

Lake Ontario

Boston

Milwaukee

Detroit

Buffalo

New York

Des Moines

Chicago

Cleveland

Harrisburg

Philadelphia

Fort Wayne

Columbus

Pittsburgh

Springfield

Indianapolis

Cincinnati

Washington, D.C.

Topeka

Louisville

Evansville

KENTUCKY

VIRGINIA

Richmond

Norfolk

ATLANTIC OCEAN

MISSOURI

Cairo

TENNESSEE

NORTH CAROLINA

New Bern

ARKANSAS

SOUTH CAROLINA

Atlanta

Charleston

MISSISSIPPI

ALABAMA

GEORGIA

TEXAS

LOUISIANA

Jackson

Port Arthur

New Orleans

Mobile

Jacksonville

FLORIDA

Gulf of Mexico

0   150   300 Miles
0   150   300 Kilometers

N
W   E
S

© SF

Where Slaves Lived in 1860

More than 50% of the people were slaves

30% to 50% of the people were slaves

10% to 30% of the people were slaves

Less than 10% of the people were slaves

No slaves, or no figures on slaves available

Main routes of the Underground Railroad

This map shows where slaves lived in 1860. In what states did most slaves live? Was the North entirely free from slavery? Trace the main routes of the Underground Railroad. To what northern cities did these routes lead?

asked Congress or the states to pass the laws they wanted. (2) They worked to elect lawmakers who agreed with their goals. (3) They talked directly to lawmakers, urging them to pass wanted laws.

Among the people. To get people to back their ideas, the abolitionists used two main tactics. (1) They held meetings, often in churches, and explained why slavery should be ended. (2) They printed newspapers and books describing the horrors of slavery. Both tactics aimed to win new members for the groups.

At meetings, former slaves might speak. People like Frederick Douglass and Sojourner [sō'jẽrn'ər] Truth described their lives as slaves. In most cases, such meetings ended with leaders asking those present who had not already done so to join their group.

Newspapers like *The Liberator*, begun by William Lloyd Garrison in 1831, tried to bring new members into the abolitionist groups. In 1833, Garrison helped found the American Anti-Slavery Society and used his paper to win new members. By 1840, the Society had almost 2,000 branches and about 200,000 members.

Direct action. Some abolitionists helped free slaves directly. A few bought slaves and freed them. More commonly, though, they helped escaping slaves by getting them into states where slavery was against the law. For example, Harriet Tubman, a runaway slave, returned to the South 19 times to lead more than 300 slaves to freedom in the North.

Tubman used a system called the Underground Railroad to free other slaves. It was a series of secret routes over which slaves traveled to freedom. The "conductors" were people like Tubman, who led the slaves to freedom. The "stations" were homes where escaping slaves could hide during the day. The runaways traveled by night, using the North Star and the Big Dipper to help lead their way.

Leaders

The antislavery groups drew most of their members from the North, but some southerners also joined. Women and men, blacks and whites—all were found in these groups.

The best-known black leader was Frederick Douglass. Born a slave, he escaped to the North and became a powerful

HARRIET TUBMAN
(1820?–1913)

The best-known black woman of the 1800s and also one of the most courageous was Harriet Tubman She gained fame through her work as a "conductor" on the Underground Railroad.

Born on a plantation in Maryland, Tubman spent her early years working in the fields or as a laborer. She became known for her great strength. Stories say she could pull fully loaded wagons.

While a slave, Tubman dreamed of freedom. Her religious faith supported this idea—all human beings were equal in the sight of God. In 1849, she escaped to Philadelphia with the help of friendly Quakers who ran the Underground Railroad. Soon she came to be a conductor on that line. She returned to the South 19 times, eventually bringing some 300 people to freedom. She became so famous that slave owners put a price of $40,000 on her head. Chased by slave catchers many times, she was never caught.

When war broke out, she served as a spy, a nurse, and a cook for the Union army. People called her "General Tubman." Honored by many Americans as a real hero, in later years she set up a home for poor black people in Auburn, New York.

speaker. One of the few black women who became speakers was Sojourner Truth, who bore 13 children in slavery before escaping. Both she and Douglass worked to end slavery in peaceful ways, but not all abolitionists did. David Walker, a free black living in Boston, wrote a booklet called *Walker's Appeal* in 1829. He said slaves should use force if that was the only way to become free. "Kill or be killed," he advised.

The American Anti-Slavery Society did not let women join. For that reason, women formed their own groups. Two of their most important leaders were Sarah and Angelina Grimké [grim kā]. Members of a rich slaveholding family, the Grimkés were from Charleston, South Carolina. They had to leave town after Angelina wrote a book in 1836 asking southern white women to fight slavery.

The Grimké sisters spoke at meetings in the North, becoming the first American women to speak before men's groups. This was so shocking at the time that Boston's ministers spoke out against it. As a result, some women abolitionists turned to working for women's rights.

White men other than Garrison who led antislavery groups included Benjamin Lundy and Theodore Weld. Lundy was a New Jersey Quaker who owned a newspaper in Baltimore in the 1820s. Garrison worked for him for a while before starting *The Liberator*. Weld was a preacher who inspired many people to become abolitionists.

Results

At first, white Americans—North and South—thought the abolitionists were **fanatics**, or extremists. But when some southerners tried to stop antislavery people from being heard, many northerners began to believe that slaveholders were trying to hide the truth. For example, in 1836, southerners pushed through a "gag rule" in the House of Representatives. This rule said that the House would not even discuss any petitions about ending the slave trade.

The abolitionists appealed to people's sense of what was fair. In the long run, they gained many followers.

SECTION 1 REVIEW
1. What tactics did abolitionists use in dealing with governments?
2. What tactics did they use to gain more followers?
3. What tactics did each of the following use: William Lloyd Garrison, Angelina Grimké, Harriet Tubman?
4. Which tactic do you think was most successful?

SECTION 2 Compromises

By 1850, many Americans had a stronger feeling of sectionalism than of nationalism. That is, they had stronger loyalties to their section than to the country as a whole. This fact affected the choices they made, for they often thought in terms of what was best for their section rather than for the whole country. In trying to decide what to do about the western lands, leaders thought about their sections as they debated two questions:

1. Should slavery be allowed in the new lands?
2. Who should decide if slavery would be allowed—Congress, the states, or the people?

The Missouri Compromise

The period after the Mexican War was not the first time Americans had faced a question about slavery in territories. Thirty years earlier, in 1819, eleven states allowed slavery and eleven states outlawed slavery. That meant there was a **balance of power** between slave states and free states. Whenever Congress voted on a law about slaves, the votes in the Senate were even and no laws passed. Then Missouri asked to enter the Union as a slave state. Congress tried to decide what to do. Neither the slave states nor the free states wanted the other side to have more votes. Finally, Henry Clay worked out a compromise that both sides could accept. (See map below.) His compromise had three points.

1. Missouri entered the Union as a slave state.
2. Maine entered the Union as a free state.
3. In the future, except for Missouri, slavery would not be allowed in the Louisiana Purchase north of 36°30′.

The Missouri Compromise, 1820

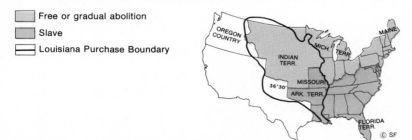

Free or gradual abolition
Slave
Louisiana Purchase Boundary

balance of power
secede
fugitive
popular sovereignty

(Above) this newspaper drawing expresses an antislavery view. (Below) this is a map of the Missouri Compromise. Find the 36°30′ line on the map. The Michigan Territory was already closed to slavery under the Northwest Ordinance. What other territory north of the line was now closed to slavery? Did Missouri lie north or south of this line? Which territories south of the line might be expected to enter the Union as slave states?

93

Abolitionists said that the Fugitive Slave Law and advertisements like this encouraged traders to cross the Ohio River, kidnap free blacks, and sell them as slaves.

The map at the right shows the balance of free and slave states and territories reached through the Compromise of 1850. Did California enter the Union as a free or a slave state? How would the question of slavery be decided in the Utah and New Mexico territories?

Congress passed the Missouri Compromise in 1820. From then until 1850, whenever Congress admitted a slave state, it soon admitted a free state, to keep the balance of power.

The Compromise of 1850

In 1850, California asked to enter the Union as a free state. The slave states objected for two reasons. First, this would destroy the balance of power, for the slave states would no longer have an equal voice in the Senate. Second, most of the new western land was north of the Missouri Compromise line of 36°30'. If the slave states let California enter as a free state, never again would they have the power to block votes on slavery. The slave states threatened to **secede**, or leave the Union, if California entered as a free state.

Once again, Henry Clay worked out a compromise. Once more, both sides were willing to give a little to keep the Union together. The Compromise of 1850 had five main parts.

1. California entered the Union as a free state.
2. Congress passed a new law dealing with runaway slaves.
3. Congress described the Texas boundaries and set up the New Mexico and Utah territories.
4. Congress repealed the Missouri Compromise line in these new territories by letting the territories decide whether to allow slavery.
5. Congress outlawed the slave trade, but not slavery, in Washington, D.C.

Compromise of 1850

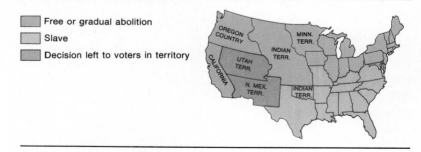

Free or gradual abolition

Slave

Decision left to voters in territory

The slave states agreed to the compromise mostly because of the new Fugitive Slave Law. It said that **fugitive**, or runaway, slaves had to be returned to their owners. Also, a person who helped a runaway escape could be fined or put into jail. This law greatly angered abolitionists.

94

The Kansas-Nebraska Act

The fuss over this compromise had hardly died down when Senator Stephen A. Douglas of Illinois stirred it up again. Like many other leaders, Douglas wanted to see a railroad built westward to the Pacific. In fact, in 1853, the United States bought a chunk of flat land—the Gadsden Purchase—from Mexico for this purpose. To build the railroad west from Chicago, as Douglas wanted, the lands west of Illinois had to be closed to Indians and organized into territories.

Douglas proposed the Kansas-Nebraska Act. Passed by Congress in 1854, it had three main points.

1. Kansas and Nebraska territories were formed.
2. **Popular sovereignty**—a vote of the people—would determine if slavery was allowed in new territories.
3. The Missouri Compromise line was abolished.

Kansas-Nebraska Act, 1854

- Free or gradual abolition
- Slave
- Decision left to voters in territory

Compare this map showing the Kansas-Nebraska Act of 1854 with the one opposite showing the Compromise of 1850. How did the Kansas-Nebraska Act change the balance between free and slave territories? Were the Kansas and Nebraska territories admitted with or without slavery? What happened to the Indian Territory?

The passage of the Kansas-Nebraska Act brought results that leaders had not foreseen. Both proslavery and abolitionist groups rushed to gain control of the Kansas Territory. War broke out between them, and about 200 people died. Finally, federal troops were sent into Kansas to keep the peace. Although not what Douglas intended, the Kansas-Nebraska Act kept slavery alive as a hot issue.

SECTION 2 REVIEW

1. Why was slavery in new lands a major question between 1820 and 1854?
2. How did sectionalism play a part in decisions about slavery?
3. What were the provisions of the Missouri Compromise? The Compromise of 1850?
4. Why did Douglas want to organize lands west of Illinois?
5. Give two results of the Kansas-Nebraska Act.

CHAPTER 20 ACTIVITIES

Wordpower!

In your own words, define each of these terms:
1. abolitionist
2. tactic
3. secede
4. balance of power
5. popular sovereignty

Reading Skills

In each pair below, identify which is the <u>cause</u> and which is the <u>effect</u>.
1. slavery/abolitionists
2. slaves freed/Underground Railroad
3. Missouri Compromise/sectionalism
4. desire for a railroad/Kansas-Nebraska Act
5. Kansas-Nebraska Act/fighting in Kansas

Writing Skills

When people on both sides of an issue have strong beliefs, working out a compromise is not easy. Select a current issue. Then write out a three- or four-point compromise. In a few sentences for each point, explain why both sides should accept it.

Figure It Out

Government and business leaders today often use a decision tree to help them make decisions. You can use one to outline a problem and reach a decision.

For example, Maria Lopez won $25,000 in a grocery-store contest. To help her decide what to do with the money, she wrote out the decision tree at right. Read it from the bottom up.

The trunk, or <u>occasion for decision</u>, was her winning the money. The branches reach toward her <u>goals</u>: "to provide for a secure future" (Goal I) or "to live for today" (Goal II).

She had many <u>alternatives</u> (shown as branches), but she considered only five: (A) put the money into a savings bank, (B) pay for more schooling, (C) start a small business, (D) buy a big car, and (E) take a trip to Europe.

Each alternative had several <u>consequences</u> (thinner branches); Alternative A had these:
1. If she needed it, the money would be there.
2. She would not have any fun with the money.

If she chose Alternative B, she would face these consequences:
1. Paying for schooling would take all the money.
2. She would prepare for a higher-paying job.

Figure out a main positive and negative consequence for her other alternatives. Then make a decision tree showing the choices Congress faced in 1850 regarding the admission of California. What alternatives did Congress have, and what could be the main positive and negative consequence of each alternative? These are the goals of the decision: "Keep the Union together," or "Let the slave states secede."

Maria Lopez's Decision Tree

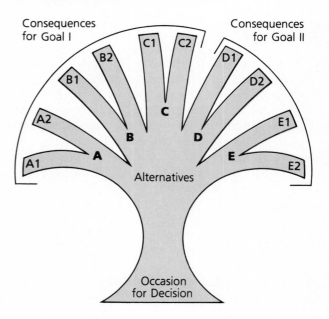

Consequences for Goal I

Consequences for Goal II

Alternatives

Occasion for Decision

CHAPTER 21

The Failure of Politics

During the 1850s, the United States moved closer and closer to **civil war**. The two sections, North and South, were like brothers arguing, yet no one knew how to stop them. This chapter deals with their quarrels. In Section 1, you will read about events that caused tension. In Section 2, you will study the elections of the 1850s. In Section 3, you will read what led Americans into war.

Glossary terms

civil war
martyr

SECTION 1 Trouble

Many events between 1850 and 1860 helped increase tension between the North and South. You have already read about some of them. The time line below shows when events took place.

Events of the 1850s

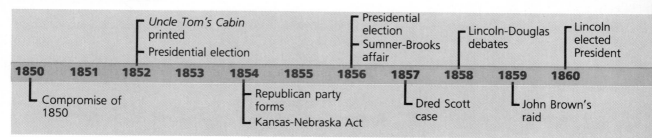

Words and Writing

Books, plays, and papers printed in the North and South kept feelings stirred up. The most important of these was *Uncle Tom's Cabin* by Harriet Beecher Stowe, printed as a book in 1852. In one year, 300,000 copies were sold. It was also made into a play that spread Stowe's ideas widely.

The book described slavery in brutal terms. The book's hero was Uncle Tom, a slave who tried to live up to the Christian ideal of turning the other cheek to his enemies. Bossing him was Simon Legree, a white overseer who used a whip freely to force slaves to do his bidding. The most dramatic part of the book had Legree hunting and chasing an

HARRIET BEECHER STOWE
(1811–1896)

During the Civil War, President Lincoln was introduced to a small woman of about 50. Looking down at her, Lincoln said, "So this is the little lady who made the big war." He had just met Harriet Beecher Stowe, who wrote *Uncle Tom's Cabin*. Her book played a big part in bringing on the Civil War.

Stowe came from one of the most famous families in America. Her father, Lyman Beecher, was one of the great preachers of the time. Her brothers and sisters became leaders in reform work.

When she was 22, her family moved to Cincinnati, Ohio. There, on the border between the slave and free states, she saw the slave system at work, and she was horrified.

Years later, after she had married, she had a vision of a scene from her days in Ohio. It was of an old black slave being beaten to death. She scribbled a description on a scrap of paper. Later, her husband found it and suggested she write a story around it. The story was *Uncle Tom's Cabin*.

escaping slave, Eliza, with dogs to the icy shores of the Ohio River.

Stowe's book appeared shortly after the Fugitive Slave Law went into force, and the story about Eliza drew attention to the new law. Many northerners objected to the law because it did not let captured blacks protect themselves. A free black who had been captured could be enslaved if a slaveholder swore that the captured black was his or her slave. Also, no trials were held to determine if captured blacks were free or slave. One word from a white slaveholder could enslave a black person who had been free from birth.

Sumner-Brooks Affair

The growing tension even touched Congress. In May, 1856, Senator Charles Sumner of Massachusetts spoke on the "Crime Against Kansas." In his speech he attacked slavery, but his words also attacked a southern senator, Andrew Butler, who was not present.

Butler's nephew, Representative Preston Brooks of South Carolina, heard about the speech. To defend his uncle's honor, Brooks entered the Senate and beat Sumner with his cane. Seriously injured, Sumner remained out of the Senate for three years.

Brooks became a hero to many in the South for his defense of his uncle, but many in the North saw him as a bully. On the other hand, Sumner became a **martyr** to many in the North. His empty seat reminded them of southern brutality.

Dred Scott Case

Another source of tension was a court case—the Dred Scott decision. Dred Scott, a slave in Missouri, had been taken into free territory by his owner. He later sued his owner to force the owner to free him, saying that since he had lived in a free territory he was free. His case went to the Supreme Court, which had to rule on two questions: (1) Was Scott a citizen and able to sue for his freedom? (2) Was Scott free because he had lived in a free territory?

Chief Justice Roger Taney gave the Court's decision in 1857. He said that the Supreme Court did not have power to hear the case. Under Missouri law, no slave was a citizen, and, therefore, no slave could sue for freedom. However, Taney then added that if the Court did have power it would rule that: (1) Slaves were property, and the 5th Amendment protected property. Therefore, slaves could be taken

anywhere, even into a free territory, and still remain slaves. (2) The Missouri Compromise had been unconstitutional because it took property away from slave owners.

The decision of the Court outraged abolitionists. They feared that slavery would now spread throughout the country. White southerners, on the other hand, felt that they had been proven right. Most important of all, the Court's decision made it very hard for law makers to work out any new compromise.

John Brown's Raid

Another event on which the North and South took different views happened in Virginia. It was the work of John Brown, a radical white abolitionist who had killed proslavery people in Kansas. In 1859, he worked out a plan to raid an arsenal in Harpers Ferry, Virginia, get guns and ammunition, and arm the slaves. Brown hoped that the slaves would revolt and win their freedom.

Brown's raid failed, and he and his followers were captured. Put on trial, Brown was sentenced to hang. The reaction in the North was one of outrage. Many northerners viewed John Brown as a martyr. Whites in the South were astonished. How could a man who wanted slaves to kill their owners be a hero? Many southerners felt that Brown was a madman, and they could not understand the reaction of the North.

Eliza crosses the Ohio River. Advertisements like this one for the play *Uncle Tom's Cabin* usually showed Eliza with light skin.

Reading Skills

Review the passage on the Dred Scott decision on page 98 to choose the correct answer for each of the following:
1. The Court ruled that:
   a. slaves were property
   b. it did not have power to hear the case
2. The decision "outraged abolitionists" because:
   a. it was hard for lawmakers to work out a new compromise
   b. they were afraid slavery would spread

SECTION 1 REVIEW

1. What view of slavery did *Uncle Tom's Cabin* give?
2. The North and the South reacted strongly to many events in the 1850s. Copy the headings below, and complete the chart.

Event	Northern Reaction	Southern Reaction
Sumner-Brooks Affair		
Dred Scott Case		
John Brown's Raid		

3. Which event in this section do you think was the most important? Explain why.

SECTION 2 Elections

In a democratic country, people try to work out their disagreements peacefully. This might be done by voting or by peaceful protests, but people try not to fight.

The elections from 1848 to 1860 reflected how Americans thought about slavery. None really settled the disagreements between North and South. Read the Reading Skills questions, study the election maps, and answer these questions.

Questions

1. Did the voters in any one section strongly favor one party over another in the election of 1848? In 1852? In 1856? In 1860?
2. Which party or parties did the southern states support in the election of 1848? In 1852? In 1856? In 1860?
3. Which party or parties did the northern states support in the election of 1848? In 1852? In 1856? In 1860?
4. In the four elections shown, which Presidents did not win a majority of the people's votes?
5. After 1852, the Whig party fell apart over the issue of slavery.
   a. What two parties appeared to take the place of the Whigs?
   b. The Republican party was against slavery. Who do you think southern Whigs supported in the election of 1856?
6. Just as questions about slavery caused the Whig party to fall apart, other parties split up or fell apart over this issue. In the election of 1860, what party split apart? What party disappeared?
7. The Constitutional Union party wanted to ignore the issue of slavery. Which states backed this party in 1860? Why do you think these particular states would want to ignore the question?
8. How did sectionalism affect the parties between 1848 and 1860?

Reading Skills

Examine the maps and charts on page 101 and choose the correct ending for each of the following:

1. The numbers on the maps represent:
   a. number of electoral votes in each state
   b. percentage of voters
   c. number of voters
2. In the charts, the numbers in the left column represent:
   a. electoral vote by state
   b. electoral votes for a candidate
   c. popular votes per state
3. The numbers in the right-hand column represent:
   a. number of electoral votes per candidate
   b. number of votes per state
   c. number of popular votes for each candidate
4. The sections in the circle charts represent:
   a. percentage of popular vote
   b. percentage of popular vote for each candidate
   c. percentage of the electoral vote

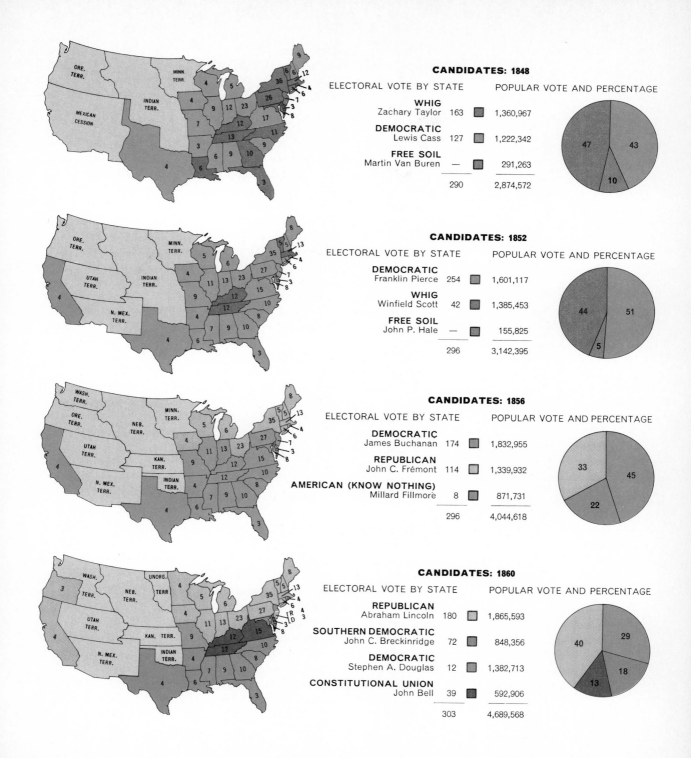

CANDIDATES: 1848

ELECTORAL VOTE BY STATE

POPULAR VOTE AND PERCENTAGE

WHIG
Zachary Taylor 163 — 1,360,967

DEMOCRATIC
Lewis Cass 127 — 1,222,342

FREE SOIL
Martin Van Buren — — 291,263

290   2,874,572

Pie: 47, 43, 10

CANDIDATES: 1852

ELECTORAL VOTE BY STATE

POPULAR VOTE AND PERCENTAGE

DEMOCRATIC
Franklin Pierce 254 — 1,601,117

WHIG
Winfield Scott 42 — 1,385,453

FREE SOIL
John P. Hale — — 155,825

296   3,142,395

Pie: 44, 51, 5

CANDIDATES: 1856

ELECTORAL VOTE BY STATE

POPULAR VOTE AND PERCENTAGE

DEMOCRATIC
James Buchanan 174 — 1,832,955

REPUBLICAN
John C. Frémont 114 — 1,339,932

AMERICAN (KNOW NOTHING)
Millard Fillmore 8 — 871,731

296   4,044,618

Pie: 33, 45, 22

CANDIDATES: 1860

ELECTORAL VOTE BY STATE

POPULAR VOTE AND PERCENTAGE

REPUBLICAN
Abraham Lincoln 180 — 1,865,593

SOUTHERN DEMOCRATIC
John C. Breckinridge 72 — 848,356

DEMOCRATIC
Stephen A. Douglas 12 — 1,382,713

CONSTITUTIONAL UNION
John Bell 39 — 592,906

303   4,689,568

Pie: 40, 29, 18, 13

The Lincoln-Douglas Debates

Questions about slavery arose in congressional elections as well as in those for President. In 1858, the election to choose a senator in Illinois interested people all over the country. The candidates were Stephen A. Douglas and Abraham Lincoln. Douglas, a Democrat, had proposed the Kansas-Nebraska Act. Lincoln, a former Whig, had the backing of the new Republican party.

Lincoln and Douglas faced one another in seven debates in different parts of Illinois. Huge crowds listened to the tall, friendly Lincoln and the short, dignified Douglas argue about slavery. Lincoln wanted to keep slavery out of the territories, while Douglas was for popular sovereignty. Lincoln said that popular sovereignty would spread slavery. Douglas said that the people in the states, not Congress, should decide if they wanted slaves.

Although Lincoln lost, he won a great deal of attention. Republicans viewed him as a possible candidate for President. White southerners viewed him and his party with fear.

SECTION 2 REVIEW

1. Who was elected President in 1848? In 1852?
2. Why were the Lincoln-Douglas debates in 1858 important?
3. By 1860, which party was antislavery? What views did the other parties have?
4. What evidence in the book agrees with the statement that parties divided along sectional lines in the 1850s?

Glossary terms

Confederacy
confiscate

SECTION 3 Secession and War

During the campaign of 1860, many southerners had said that their states would secede from the Union if Lincoln was elected President. They feared that he would end slavery, despite his promise that his views about slavery dealt with the territories, not the states. They believed that states' rights, guaranteed by the Constitution, allowed the states to decide if people could have slaves.

Lincoln was so unpopular in the South that in the 1860 presidential election, he did not receive a single vote in ten southern states. Out of 1,865,593 votes for Lincoln, only 27,000 were cast in the slave states. After the events of the 1850s, many southerners were sure that the North, and the Republican party, wished to destroy the South.

Secession

In December, 1860, the South Carolina legislature led the way for the South by voting to secede from the Union. By February, 1861, six other states had followed. They were Georgia, Florida, Alabama, Mississippi, Louisiana, and Texas.

These seven states sent representatives to meet in Montgomery, Alabama. In February, 1861, they formed a new government for the South called the Confederate States of America or the **Confederacy**. They began writing a constitution, much like the United States Constitution, but with one exception—they did not allow laws against slavery. They chose Jefferson Davis of Louisiana to be president of the Confederacy and Alexander Stephens of Georgia to be vice-president. They also **confiscated**, or took over, all of the property belonging to the United States government. This included post offices, mints (where money is made), and forts.

During this time, James Buchanan was still President of the United States. Lincoln would not be sworn in as President until March 4, 1861.

Buchanan took no action against the southern states. Historians give three reasons for this: (1) Buchanan believed that the states had no right to leave the Union, but he did not think the central government had the right to use force against them. (2) Buchanan was afraid that using force would cause the slave states still in the Union to secede. (3) Buchanan did not want to be remembered as the President who started a civil war.

Fort Sumter

When Lincoln became President on March 4, 1861, he told Americans that he would "hold, occupy, and possess" all property that belonged to the federal government. Lincoln went on to say that he would preserve the Union at all cost, but that if fighting was to start, the South would have to start it.

By April, 1861, the country was like a powder keg waiting to explode. All that was needed was a spark to light the fuse. Fort Sumter, on an island in the harbor of Charleston, South Carolina, provided that spark.

The fort's commander, Major Robert Anderson, refused to give up Fort Sumter to the Confederacy. Confederate President Davis then ordered General Pierre Beauregard to take

ABRAHAM LINCOLN
(1809–1865)

Of all the American Presidents, Abraham Lincoln is probably the one who has been most loved and most hated. Because he led the country through a civil war, few Americans of the time had neutral feelings about him.

Lincoln was born in a log cabin in Kentucky to a poor farming family. His mother died when he was nine, and his father kept moving west in search of a better life. From Kentucky, the family moved to Indiana and then to Illinois.

Abraham's mother had given her son a love for reading, even though she did not know how to read. Mainly self-taught, young Abraham worked on the farm until he was 22, then moved on. He worked on boats on the Mississippi before settling in New Salem, Illinois. There, he kept a store and studied law.

Lincoln worked hard to get ahead. Eventually, he became a member of the Illinois legislature and then the U.S. Congress.

Lincoln spoke out against slavery. He helped found a new political party that agreed with his ideas. The Republican party nominated him for President in 1860, but when he won, civil war became certain. Through four years of war, Lincoln held the Union together. With war's end, a fanatic killed him.

The Union and the Confederacy, 1861

Legend:
- Free states and territories
- Slave states loyal to the Union
- Confederate states of America
- Territory supporting the Confederacy

This map shows the Union and the Confederacy in 1861. West Virginia seceded from Virginia in 1861 and was admitted to the Union in 1863. The Indian Territory (shown in brown) did not have a unified government—some tribes backed the Union, some, the Confederacy. Study the map. Which states and territories formed the Union? Which formed the Confederacy?

Reading Skills

Read the second paragraph under "Fort Sumter" on page 103 to determine the meaning of the following figurative terms:
1. "powder keg"
   a. Fort Sumter   b. United States
2. "spark"
   a. an event   b. an island
3. "light the fuse"
   a. explode   b. start the war

the fort. Beauregard waited, hoping that Anderson, who was an old friend, would surrender. Anderson, with 65 starving men, was no match for Beauregard and his 5,000 Confederate troops, but he would not give up.

On April 12, 1861, Beauregard gave the command to fire on the fort. After two days of shelling, Anderson surrendered. No soldiers had been killed, but a long bloody war—the Civil War—had begun.

Lincoln called for 75,000 volunteers to join the army. The South also called for volunteers. As the war began, four more slave states left the Union: Virginia, North Carolina, Tennessee, and Arkansas. Four other slave states—those on the border between North and South—stayed in the Union. They were Missouri, Kentucky, Maryland, and Delaware.

SECTION 3 REVIEW

1. Why did southern states fear Lincoln and the Republicans?
2. How soon after Lincoln's election did South Carolina vote to secede?
3. Why did Buchanan refuse to use force against the seceding states?
4. What was the Confederate States of America?
5. Do you think a state should be allowed to leave the Union if it wants? Give reasons for your answer.

CHAPTER 21 ACTIVITIES

Wordpower!

Unscramble each term in capital letters in the sentences below to spell out words from this chapter.

1. In a VILIC RAW people from the same country fight over who will govern them.
2. Someone who gives his or her life for a great cause or idea is a TYRMAR.
3. The southern states said that TATESS' THRIGS guaranteed by the Constitution allowed them to decide if they would allow slavery or not.
4. In 1861, the southern states formed the FEDCONCYRAE.
5. The government in the South ordered its troops to CAFISCONTE Union property.

Reading Skills

Re-read the chapter introduction to choose the correct answer below:

1. A word that means the North and South is:
   a. events   b. brothers   c. elections
2. A word that means conflicts is:
   a. events   b. quarrels   c. elections

Writing Skills

This chapter describes several events—the printing of *Uncle Tom's Cabin*, the Dred Scott decision, the Lincoln-Douglas debates—that increased hatred between people who were for or against slavery. Write a one-paragraph essay explaining how each side reacted to three or four of the events described in this chapter.

Figure It Out

The Civil War did not just happen. Many of the events you read about in Units 6 and 7 were causes of the war. Copy the chart at right. Next to each cause listed, check whether you think it was an underlying cause, an immediate cause, or a spark. Then list the reason for your choice.

Causes of the Civil War	Immediate Cause	Underlying Cause	Spark	Reason for Your Choice
Slavery				
Work of abolitionists to end slavery				
Defense of slavery by white southerners				
Addition of new lands after the Mexican War				
Sectionalism				
North supported high tariffs, factories				
South wanted low tariffs, more land for plantations				
States' rights				
The South favored the right of states to pass laws that preserved its way of life				
The North opposed laws that let states go against the wishes of Congress				
Fanatics and the decisions of leaders				
Polk's policy of expansion				
Sumner-Brooks affair				
Uncle Tom's Cabin				
John Brown's raid				
Compromise of 1850				
Kansas-Nebraska Act				
Election of Lincoln				
Buchanan's refusal to act to stop secessionists				
Lincoln's insistence on preserving the Union				
The bombing of Fort Sumter				

UNIT 7 TEST

In your notebook, write the answers to the following questions.

Completion

Fill in each blank with the term that best completes the sentence.

Fugitive	manifest
secede	annex
emigrant	abolitionist
sovereignty	

1. The idea of _____ destiny was that it was God's will for the United States to grow.
2. An _____ is a person who moves from one place to another within a country.
3. The Texas legislature asked the United States to _____ Texas.
4. An _____ was a person who wanted to end slavery.
5. The slave states threatened to _____, or leave, the Union if California entered as a free state.
6. Popular _____ was the idea that voters should decide whether or not slavery would be allowed.
7. The _____ Slave Law provided for runaway slaves to be returned to their owners.

Multiple Choice

Choose the ending that best completes each sentence.

1. Emigrants crossed the plains on the Oregon Trail to reach:
   a. the Mississippi Valley
   b. the Nueces Valley
   c. the Willamette Valley
2. The saying "54-40 or Fight" referred to:
   a. Oregon
   b. Texas
   c. California
3. The first president of the Texas Republic was:
   a. Sam Houston
   b. Stephen Austin
   c. Santa Anna
4. The question decided by the election of 1844 was about:
   a. slavery
   b. expansion
   c. voting
5. The United States and Mexico both claimed the land:
   a. between the Mississippi and the Hudson
   b. between the Rio Grande and the Nueces
   c. between the Columbia and the Willamette
6. The Mexican War ended with the:
   a. Treaty of Monterrey
   b. Treaty of Chapultepec
   c. Treaty of Guadalupe Hidalgo
7. Abolitionist tactics included all of the following except:
   a. signing petitions
   b. passing amendments
   c. holding meetings
   d. buying slaves and freeing them
8. The Underground Railroad:
   a. ran on rails underground
   b. brought slaves from the North to the South
   c. smuggled escaping slaves out of the South
9. the Missouri Compromise was reached:
   a. in 1820
   b. in 1850
   c. in 1854
10. California entered the Union through:
    a. the Missouri Compromise
    b. the Compromise of 1850
    c. the Kansas-Nebraska Act
11. The author of Uncle Tom's Cabin was:
    a. Harriet Tubman
    b. Harriet Beecher Stowe
    c. Harriet Whitman

12. John Brown attacked Harpers Ferry:
    a. to get weapons for a slave revolt
    b. to free Jefferson Davis
    c. to uphold Sumner's honor
13. The Lincoln-Douglas debates brought attention to the policies of:
    a. the Free Soil party
    b. the Know-Nothing party
    c. the Republican party
14. The first southern state to vote to secede was:
    a. South Carolina
    b. Georgia
    c. Tennessee
15. The Civil War began with:
    a. the Missouri Compromise
    b. the shelling of Fort Sumter
    c. the election of Lincoln

Reading Graphic Aids

Match the letter on the time line to the event listed for that year.
1. Civil War begins
2. Kansas-Nebraska Act
3. Dred Scott decision
4. *Uncle Tom's Cabin* printed
5. California enters Union
6. John Brown's raid on Harpers Ferry
7. Lincoln-Douglas debates
8. Lincoln elected President

A   B   C   D E F G H

1850   1855   1860

Fact or Opinion

Write "F" if a statement is a fact, "O" if it is opinion.
1. "Oregon fever" was the urge to move to the Oregon Country.
2. Mexico should not have tried to keep Texas.
3. The abolitionists were fanatics.
4. Abolitionists tried many tactics to end slavery.
5. Stephen Douglas wanted to build a railroad, not start a war.
6. The Civil War was fought between the North and the South.
7. The South did the right thing by voting to leave the Union.
8. The war could have been avoided if slavery had been abolished.
9. Abraham Lincoln was a better President than Jefferson Davis.
10. The war began at Fort Sumter, South Carolina.

Essay

The authors titled this unit "The Path to Disunion." You could call the events described in this unit <u>steps</u> toward disunion. What three or four such <u>steps</u> were most important? Write a one-paragraph essay giving a reason or two for each of your choices.

UNIT 8

The Battle of Fredericksburg, 1862,
painted by John Richards

WAR AND PEACE
1861–1877

In 1861, the United States split in two, and the North and the South went to war with one another. Nothing about the war was simple—not the causes, not the events, not the results. In fact, Americans even disagree over the name of the war. Although it is now usually called the Civil War, it is also known as the War Between the States, the War of the Rebellion, and the War of Northern Aggression.

The Civil War left much history for later generations. It left heroes such as Abraham Lincoln, Robert E. Lee, Ulysses S. Grant, "Stonewall" Jackson, and others less famous from both the North and the South—civilians and soldiers, blacks and whites, men and women.

It also left questions. Probably more books have been written and read about the American Civil War than any other subject in American history. Many people still debate or talk about the war. "What if" questions are often heard. What if Lincoln had not been elected? What if Lee had stayed with the Union? What if . . . ? The questions go on and on.

What is certain is that the war was costly, in both money and lives. More than 600,000 Americans died in the Civil War. The ruin of the land, particularly in the South, would take many years to mend.

The war was especially hard because all the soldiers, whether from the North or South, were Americans. They spoke the same language, prayed to the same God, and had many of the same customs. Think of yourself when you read about the Civil War, because it is the "average" American who fights wars and endures life on the home front.

The war lasted four years, and when it was over the South was in ruins. This Unit looks at the Civil War and the attempts to rebuild the South once it was over.

CHAPTER 22
The Civil War

CHAPTER 23
Reconstruction

TIME LINE

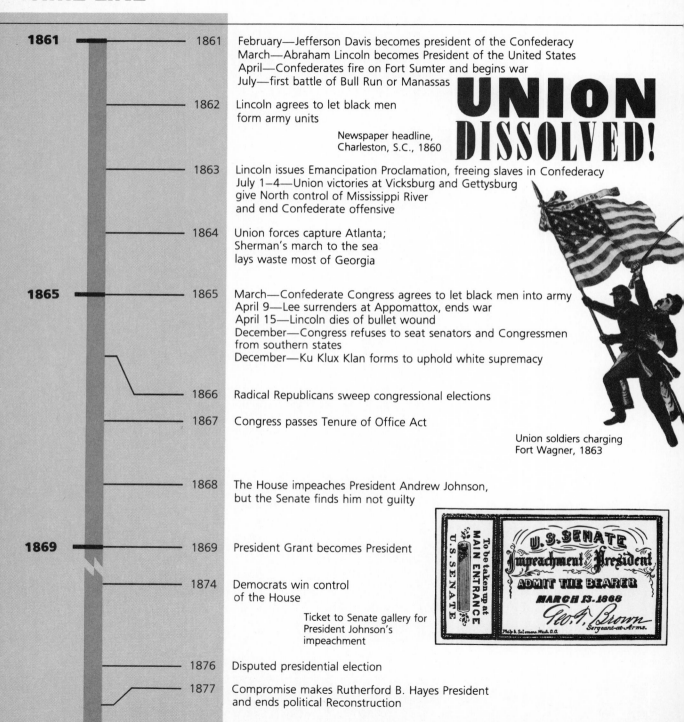

1861 — 1861 February—Jefferson Davis becomes president of the Confederacy
March—Abraham Lincoln becomes President of the United States
April—Confederates fire on Fort Sumter and begins war
July—first battle of Bull Run or Manassas

— 1862 Lincoln agrees to let black men
form army units

Newspaper headline,
Charleston, S.C., 1860

UNION DISSOLVED!

— 1863 Lincoln issues Emancipation Proclamation, freeing slaves in Confederacy
July 1–4—Union victories at Vicksburg and Gettysburg
give North control of Mississippi River
and end Confederate offensive

— 1864 Union forces capture Atlanta;
Sherman's march to the sea
lays waste most of Georgia

1865 — 1865 March—Confederate Congress agrees to let black men into army
April 9—Lee surrenders at Appomattox, ends war
April 15—Lincoln dies of bullet wound
December—Congress refuses to seat senators and Congressmen
from southern states
December—Ku Klux Klan forms to uphold white supremacy

— 1866 Radical Republicans sweep congressional elections

— 1867 Congress passes Tenure of Office Act

Union soldiers charging
Fort Wagner, 1863

— 1868 The House impeaches President Andrew Johnson,
but the Senate finds him not guilty

1869 — 1869 President Grant becomes President

— 1874 Democrats win control
of the House

Ticket to Senate gallery for
President Johnson's
impeachment

— 1876 Disputed presidential election

— 1877 Compromise makes Rutherford B. Hayes President
and ends political Reconstruction

CHAPTER 22

The Civil War

The Civil War actually began when the South fired on Fort Sumter in the harbor of Charleston, South Carolina, in April, 1861. After the shelling of Fort Sumter, President Lincoln called for 75,000 troops to defend the Union. President Davis had already called for 100,000 to uphold the Confederacy. War had begun.

Men from both the North and South flocked to join the army. Brothers took sides against each other, especially in the border states. George B. Crittenden became a general in the Confederate army, while his brother, Thomas, became a general in the Union army. Their father, John J. Crittenden of Kentucky, had worked in Congress to try to hold the country together. Friends and relatives of Abraham Lincoln fought for the South.

The Civil War was long—four years long. In this chapter you will study the highlights. You should get an idea of what the Civil War was like, for both soldiers and civilians.

Section 1 describes the resources of the two sides. Section 2 is an overview of the battles. Section 3 describes the war as soldiers saw it. Section 4 is about the home front. Section 5 describes the war's end.

A young Union soldier, painted by Winslow Homer

SECTION 1 Resources: North and South

The Civil War was a "total war." That is, it was a war that used almost all possible resources and touched civilians as well as the military. The people "back home" faced many hardships, including shortages of food and other supplies.

The war was also America's first "modern" war. Both sides used railroads to move men and supplies. They sent up balloons to observe the enemy and used the telegraph to send information about troop movements.

Before you read about the resources of the two sides, think of yourself involved in a war. What would you need to beat your enemy, and how would you get these things? Make a list of what you would need. Then study the charts, graphs, and map in this section to see what resources the North and South had at the start of the war.

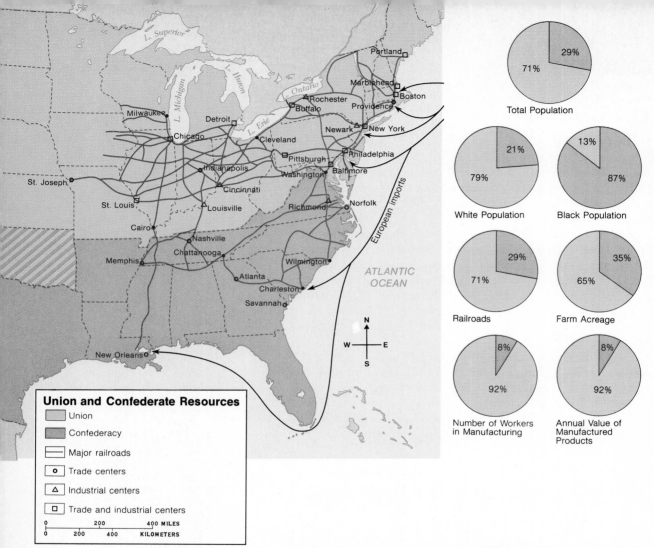

Union and Confederate Resources

- Union
- Confederacy
- Major railroads
- ○ Trade centers
- △ Industrial centers
- □ Trade and industrial centers

Total Population: 71% / 29%

White Population: 79% / 21%

Black Population: 87% / 13%

Railroads: 71% / 29%

Farm Acreage: 65% / 35%

Number of Workers in Manufacturing: 92% / 8%

Annual Value of Manufactured Products: 92% / 8%

The map, graphs, and chart on this page compare the resources of the Union and the Confederacy in some important ways. Study the page carefully and then answer the questions at the top of page 113. Use the map to locate the major railroads and the trade and industrial centers. Use the circle graphs to determine the percentage of the nation's resources controlled by the North (green) or the South (orange). Refer to the chart for a comparison of firearms and farm products.

	North	South
Manufacture of firearms	97% made	3% made
Livestock (millions)		
Horses	3–4	1.7
Cows	10–12	9.7
Agriculture (millions)		
Corn (bushels)	396	280
Wheat (bushels)	114	31
Cotton (bales)	0	5
Tobacco (pounds)	58	199
Rice (pounds)	0	187

Questions

1. Which side, the North or the South, had the largest number of people? How might this affect the outcome of the war?
2. What percentage of the nation's railroad mileage did the North have? The South? How could this affect the war effort?
3. What percentage of the nation's manufactured products did the North produce? The South? In what way could this affect the outcome of the war?
4. Tobacco and cotton were grown mainly for export. Which side grew the most of these crops? Which side grew mostly food crops? How might these differences affect the outcome of the war?
5. Which side had the most money? How might this affect the outcome of the war?
6. Which side do you think had the best chance to win the war? Give evidence to support your conclusion.

Other Advantages and Disadvantages

Not all advantages and disadvantages can be shown in charts and measured. Here are some other considerations.

The South went to war thinking it had these advantages. (1) The South was fighting for a cause: "independence" for many southerners, "southern rights," or "states' rights" for others. (2) The South was fighting a **defensive** war. Southerners thought they would need fewer soldiers because they had only to defend land, while the North had to capture and hold land. (3) Southerners knew the land better than did the northern soldiers, and they were used to the weather, particularly the hot summers. (4) Southern soldiers could shoot and ride better than northern soldiers who had lived in cities and worked in factories.

The North had these advantages. (1) The North was fighting to preserve the Union and uphold the Constitution. (2) In Lincoln, the North had a strong political leader, who learned to cope effectively with all the problems of war.

The form of government and quality of military leaders also affected the war. The United States government was stronger than the Confederate States of America. Its leaders did not have to take time while fighting a war to figure out who could or should be doing what. The Confederate constitution supported states' rights so strongly that some southern governors refused to enforce Confederate laws in their states.

At the beginning of the war, the South had the best military leaders. The brilliant military **strategies** of men like General Robert E. Lee and General "Stonewall" Jackson are

JEFFERSON DAVIS
(1809–1889)

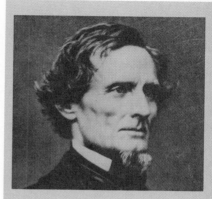

Jefferson Davis is best known as the president of the Confederate States of America during the Civil War. However, he had not wanted that job. A graduate of West Point and a veteran of the Mexican War, he wanted to be a general. This desire often interfered with his judgment in running the Confederate government.

Davis had served in the United States government before the South seceded. In 1847, Davis became a senator from Mississippi. In 1853, he was named Secretary of War, but he returned to the Senate in 1857. As a senator and cabinet officer, he pushed for southern rights in the United States government.

As president of the Confederacy, he faced strong opposition to many of his decisions. Many southerners blamed him for the South's defeat.

After the South surrendered in 1865, Davis fled southward but was captured near Irwinville, Georgia. Sent to a federal prison for two years, he came to be viewed as a martyr to the southern cause.

He settled in Mississippi in his later years and spent three years writing *The Rise and Fall of the Confederate States*, a history of the Civil War.

People base their beliefs or ideas on one or both of the following:
  a. evidence (proof, usually facts of some kind)
  b. emotion (feelings, something is right or wrong)

Of these two, emotion is often least trustworthy although it is the most widely used. Examine each of the following statements. On your paper, write "a" if the basis for a statement is evidence or "b" if the basis is emotion.

1. page 113, paragraph 3: "Southerners thought they would need fewer soldiers because they had only to defend land, while the North had to capture and hold land."
2. page 113, last paragraph: "The brilliant strategies of men like General Robert E. Lee and General 'Stonewall' Jackson are still studied today."

Glossary term

counterattack

New York's 7th Regiment marching down Broadway, April 1861

still studied today. Other southern generals were among the best to graduate from West Point, and they had gained much experience in the Mexican War. Lincoln tried a number of Union generals before he finally found, in Ulysses S. Grant, a leader who could win.

SECTION 1 REVIEW

1. Which side had the most advantages in terms of resources that can be touched and measured?
2. Which side had the most advantages in terms of factors that cannot be measured?
3. Southerners thought they had a chance to win because they had seen in the American Revolution that the winner in a war is not necessarily the best-equipped side. Compare the American Revolution (Chapter 6) to the Civil War. What advantages did Americans have in the Revolution that the South had in the Civil War?

SECTION 2 Fighting the War

The Civil War was fought mainly in the South. A battle usually lasted one to two days, and hundreds were fought. Most of the fighting was hand-to-hand combat as one side charged the other's line.

Both sides thought the war would be short. Both sides were sadly mistaken, as they learned at the first big battle of the Civil War—the first battle of Bull Run or Manassas. (Many battles have two names, because the North often named them after rivers and the South named them after towns.)

Bull Run

The battle began on July 21, 1861, a hot, sticky summer day. The town of Manassas, Virginia, near a small creek called Bull Run, was important to both sides because of its railroad lines. The town was so close to Washington, D.C., that many people came from the capital to "watch the war" from the hilltops. They wanted to witness the battle that would "end" the war. A few Union officers mixed among them to explain the battle. Some people even brought picnic lunches.

When a Union soldier reported, "We've whipped them on all points. We have taken all their batteries. They are retreating as fast as they can," a woman said, "I guess we will be in Richmond this time tomorrow."

However, the Union troops were not in Richmond the next day, nor did they win the battle. Both sides had raw, untrained troops, and both sides panicked. At first it appeared the North was winning because the Confederates retreated. Then General Thomas J. Jackson stopped the retreat by encouraging his men. A fellow officer is supposed to have said, "There stands Jackson, like a stone wall." From then on, this Confederate leader was known as "Stonewall" Jackson. The Confederates **counterattacked**, and the Union troops turned and retreated.

The northern retreat started out orderly but then became confused. Troops began running back to Washington along with the sightseers. Some soldiers threw down their supplies and guns. To add to the confusion, both sides had on similarly colored uniforms, and neither side could tell who the enemy was.

While the northern troops were confused, so were those of the South. Many historians think the South could have taken Washington, D.C., but was not organized well enough to grab the opportunity. Joseph E. Johnston, a leading Confederate commander, said the southern army was "more disorganized by victory than that of the United States by defeat."

This battle made both sides realize that the war was going to take a long time. They also saw that they needed to be better organized. Because of the battle, the South adopted gray uniforms and a new battle flag. The North kept the blue uniforms of the United States Army.

The first battle of Bull Run, also called Manassas—Virginia, July 21, 1861

Reading Skills

The sequence of events in the battle of Bull Run or Manassas can be confusing. To sort out these events, re-read the account of that battle to answer the following questions:
1. Which side was first thought to have won?
   a. neither   c. South
   b. North   d. both
2. On which side did troops retreat at some point?
   a. neither   c. South
   b. North   d. both
3. Which side was disorganized?
   a. neither   c. South
   b. North   d. both
4. Which side actually won?
   a. neither   c. South
   b. North   d. both

The Civil War

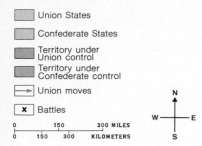

Union States

Confederate States

Territory under Union control

Territory under Confederate control

→ Union moves

✗ Battles

N
W ← → E
S

0   150   300 MILES
0   150   300 KILOMETERS

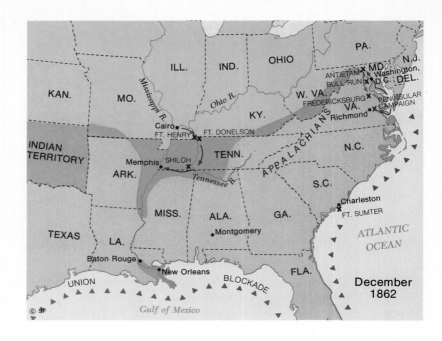

December 1862

December, 1862

The upper map on this page shows the early stages of the war. Red triangles indicate the Union blockade of southern ports, intended to keep the South from receiving imports or sending exports. In addition to the blockade, the Union hoped to divide the Confederacy by gaining control of the Mississippi River. Early Union victories at Fort Henry, Fort Donelson, and Shiloh in Tennessee were an important part of this plan. Finally, the Union hoped to capture the Confederate capital at Richmond, Virginia.

The Confederate plan was to fight a defensive war and wear down the North. The Confederates also hoped to cut off the Northeast from the rest of the Union. The South moved quickly to end the war, with its early victories in Virginia at Bull Run, in the Peninsular Campaign, and at Fredericksburg.

December, 1863

The lower map shows the war after the Union won major victories at Vicksburg, Mississippi, and Gettysburg, Pennsylvania. The victory at Vicksburg gave the Union control of the Mississippi River, splitting the South in two. The battle of Gettysburg marked the end of Confederate efforts to invade the North. At the battle of Chickamauga in northwest Georgia, Confederate forces defeated a Union army. However, the Union soon took that area.

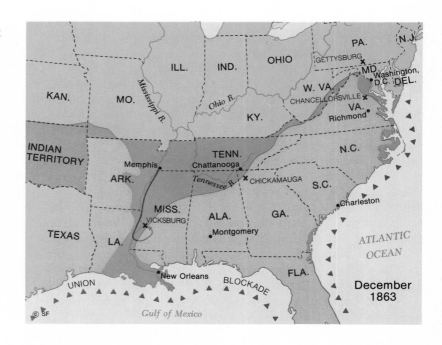

December 1863

116

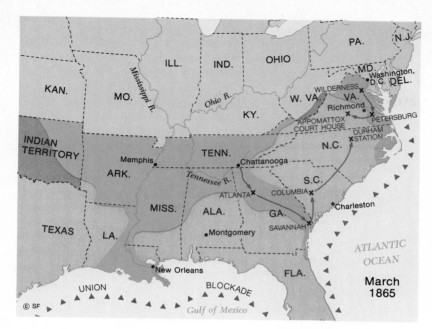

March, 1865

The map at the left shows the final stages of the Civil War. Union forces under General William T. Sherman had completed their destructive march from northwest Georgia to Savannah and the sea, then moved on north through North Carolina. The war drew to an end at Appomattox Court House in Virginia.

Examine all three maps and the table of key Civil War battles below. At which of the three periods shown on the maps was Confederate control of Union areas the greatest? At which period was Union control the greatest? Where were the major battles fought at each of the three periods shown on the maps? Which commanders on each side led the most successful actions? Which battles seem most significant?

Key Civil War Battles

Battle/Date	Northern Commander	Southern Commander	Outcome/Results
Shiloh April 6–7, 1862	Ulysses S. Grant	Albert S. Johnson	Union gains control of western Tennessee. Bloodiest battle of the war.
Seven Days' Battle May–June, 1862	George B. McClellan	Robert E. Lee	Lee outlasts McClellan; Lincoln fires McClellan as head of army.
Antietam Sept. 17, 1862	George B. McClellan	Robert E. Lee	Lee's invasion of the North is stopped.
Chancellorsville May 2–4, 1863	Joseph Hooker	Robert E. Lee	Lee defeats Hooker. Stonewall Jackson killed.
Vicksburg March–July 4, 1863	Ulysses S. Grant	John Pemberton	A siege of months starves Vicksburg into surrender. South losses control of Mississippi River.
Gettysburg July 1–3, 1863	George Meade	Robert E. Lee	North defeats South. Lee and his army escape to Virginia, never again invade the North.

SECTION 2 REVIEW

1. Judging from the maps, which side was most successful in carrying out its strategy? What evidence supports your answer?
2. In what battles was the South aiming to split the Northeast from the Northwest?
3. Why do you think both sides were so disorganized at the first battle of Bull Run?

Glossary terms

desert
conscription

(Left) Union soldiers guard equipment used by General Ulysses Grant during his military operations in the South. The photo was taken at City Point, Virginia, in 1864 by the famous Civil War photographer Mathew Brady. (Right) black soldiers prepare for battle at Johnsonville, Tennessee, in 1864.

SECTION 3 The Soldier's Life

Look around your classroom. Everyone in it is the same age as someone who took part in the Civil War. At the beginning of the war, an "old" soldier was around 30, but the average age was 18 or 19. Toward the end, southern soldiers were much younger and much older because the South began running out of young men who could fight. Drummer boys often were as young as 12. One at Shiloh was only 10.

At first, neither side allowed black men to fight. Although many black men volunteered in the North, Lincoln did not let them join the army because he thought this might cause the border states to secede. Finally, in 1862, Lincoln agreed to let black soldiers fight in the Union army but only in segregated (separate) units. Black soldiers often received less pay and poorer training and medical treatment than whites. Some

black soldiers refused their pay until it was the same as other soldiers. In 1864, Congress passed a law giving all soldiers, black or white, the same pay rates. By the end of the war, about 186,000 black soldiers had fought for the Union, and 21 received the Congressional Medal of Honor for outstanding service and bravery.

Strangely, near the end of the war, the South decided to let slaves into the Confederate army. The war ended before a plan passed by the Confederate Congress could be put into effect.

As the war dragged on, both sides needed more soldiers. Many soldiers who had first been excited about going to war soon became lonely and miserable. Many **deserted** and went home to their families.

The North and the South passed **conscription**, or draft, laws to force white men into army service. Both laws let a drafted man hire a substitute to serve in his place. Many soldiers began to feel that it was a "rich man's war and a poor man's fight." In New York, the draft was so unpopular that riots broke out in 1863. Immigrants who opposed fight-

Detail from a painting of General George Pickett's charge against the Confederates at the battle of Gettysburg, 1863

ing a war to free the slaves set fire to buildings, killed or tortured black people, and looted shops to protest being called up in the draft. About 500 persons died, and troops had to be called in to restore order.

Letters from Soldiers

What was life like for a soldier? To find out, read the following letters to Sarah Hodges Brannen from her brother James (nicknamed Jimma) and her Uncle William. As you read, consider what hardships soldiers faced and how they felt about food, mail, death, and the fighting.

SEPT. 20TH, 1861

DEAR SISTER,

Now that I have a few minutes I will try to drop you a few lines. Life is not so hard for us now. We get fairly good rations, at least for soldiers. We get cornmeal, . . . sea crackers, rice, coffee, sugar, bacon, beef, soup, and candles to burn at night if we want them. And I believe we get enough of each kind except rice.

We do not hear much news as of now. There is some news that we will be moving to Tennessee soon. I wish we were going to be closer to home, for I miss everyone so much. Please write me a letter and just write about everything you can think of. I would like very much to know how your cotton, corn, and crops turned out, how many hogs you are fattening. Oh, I tell you, almost anything would afford me a little comfort.   J. C. HODGES

P.S. Our brother Samuel is well and hearty at present. Some of the others are a little puny.

FEB. 9, 1862

DEAR SISTER,

I have concluded to write you another letter this evening but it is so late that I want to be able to finish it tonight, as our candles are very scarce. . . .

It has been quite rainy here most all day and I tell you it is a bad time to cook. For we have to cook with green wood and that right out open in the weather. . . .

Sarah, I just ate supper and we had good corn bread, fried pork, and coffee. That was pretty good for a rainy evening, wasn't it? I believe we all had enough but Uncle William. He said he wanted one more piece of fried pork. We have plenty of sweetened coffee here most any time. If I only could hand

(Top) a young Georgian soldier (Bottom) 9th Mississippi Regiment stationed in Pensacola, Florida, 1861

over my part to you, I would be glad, for I have no use for coffee myself and I expect that coffee is a great object with you all now.

It is getting so dark I shall have to stop. I've had to stand guard two hours this morning and I'll have to stand six more before tomorrow morning.

Your dearest brother, JIMMA

FEB. 12

DEAR SARAH,

I have seated myself to try to answer your valuable letter I received.

It is a cold, dull wintery time with me in many respects. In the first place, I got no encouraging news to tell you about peace from what I can learn. There is another fight pending as soon as the weather gets so we can travel, but the ground is too wet for the artillery to move and I hope it may stay so till warm weather. . . . I don't think it would be right to make us fight in such cold weather. We have got us some little houses built now and I would hate to leave this place. . . .

I think about my dear Mother, who may be at the same time lying on her bed, asking the Lord to be with her poor soldier boy and grant him safety from all harm. But think how many thousands of mothers are left at such a distance to mourn the departure of loving sons who have stepped in the field of battle to defend their rights, and many have gone in that never came out. Oh, what a sight to go into battle, to face so many men of war and they shouting their best. . . . You can hear the wounded in every direction hollering and begging for help. It's "Oh! do help me, do carry me out of this place, Oh! William, do for God's sake help me for I'm wounded and can't walk one step."

I wish I could give you my rations of flour for some potatoes. I have not had a potato since I have been in Virginia.

Your loving Uncle till death, WILLIAM

(Top) Union soldier J. L. Balldwin (Bottom) Union soldiers standing in front of the camp kitchen

NOV. 20, 1862

DEAR SARAH,

I will try to answer your kind letter, as I have just got back to my regiment. I had to witness the death of your dear brother. Sarah, I do think I loved him the best of anybody else for I have been with him so long and he had always treated me so tender and kind. Oh, he was such a good boy,

Major Belle Boyd, a famous Confederate spy

it seemed like it would almost break my heart to see him fixed in the cold clay of Maryland. I could not get a coffin to put him in, nothing but one thin blanket to wrap him in, and to see the clay piled in on his dear body. I got 2 men to dig his grave and I helped them put him in, while the tears [were] streaming from my eyes and I reckon there was more than a thousand Yankees standing around, but it gives me satisfaction to [know] that I was with him and that he lacked for nothing that I could do. I cut off a lock of his hair to send you. I would not send it all for fear the letter would be lost.

I remain as ever your sincere,   UNCLE WILLIAM

The "Enemy"

Perhaps because the soldiers were so young, they did not always consider the other side as an enemy. This is not to say all northerners liked southerners, or vice versa. Some people from both the North and the South hated each other. But it was a strange war, and people on both sides often felt some closeness to those they fought, especially at the start.

One of the most common episodes was the trading of items from one side to the other, usually tobacco for coffee. A standard exchange went like this: "Hello Yank!" "Hello, Johnny!" "Got any coffee?" "Yes. Got any tobacco?" "Yes, come and get it." "Won't shoot?" "No."

Then "Billy Yank" and "Johnny Reb" would cross the river or line of battle and make their exchanges. A northern soldier wrote in his diary, "We made a bargain with them that we would not fire on them if they would not fire on us, and they were as good as their word. They talked about their mothers, their fathers, their sweethearts, just as we did. They did not seem like the enemy."

The evening before a big battle the soldiers often would sing loud enough to be heard on the other side. Each side had favorite songs and would call them out to be sung. The next day, the men would face each other in battle.

SECTION 3 REVIEW

1. Were the writers of the Civil War letters you read from the North or the South? Give evidence to support your answer. In what ways do you think letters from a soldier on the other side might be different?

2. List three hardships soldiers faced during the Civil War.

3. Why were letters so important to soldiers?

4. Why do you think some soldiers talked with the "enemy"?

Reading Skills

Examine the listed terms and passages to determine what purpose the quotation marks serve. Is each:
   a. a quotation by someone other than the authors of the text?
   b. a special use of a word or phrase?
   c. a famous saying or a slogan?
1. (page 119, last paragraph): "a rich man's war and a poor man's fight"
2. (page 122, line 12): "enemy"
3. (page 122, line 26): "we made a bargain with them . . ."

SECTION 4 Life on the Home Front

Soldiers felt the effects of the war most strongly. The war, however, also hit people on the home fronts.

Keeping Life Going

Since so many men were away fighting, women ran farms and businesses. Many women began working in factories that made war goods. Women also took jobs in government offices.

In the North, with the help of new machinery, many women produced large crops on family farms. Without southern cotton, the cotton mills of New England produced less cloth and had less need for workers. However, a few industries in the North boomed, as the need for war supplies grew, and some people became wealthy through the war.

Because most of the war was fought in the South, people there felt the war sooner than those in the North. The South had to learn to live on less and less. Not only did the fighting destroy southern crops, but the northern blockade of southern ports cut off supplies and food. Almost as important, the South had little gold and silver to back up its money. The Confederate government printed so much paper

(Left) a southern family flees from the invading Yankees. (Right) former slaves sit in front of their quarters in Culpepper, Virginia, November, 1863.

123

Under the heading "Keeping Life Going" on page 123 are four paragraphs. Choose the best <u>main</u> <u>idea</u> for each paragraph listed:

1. Paragraph 1:
   a. Women worked in factories.
   b. Women helped by working at a variety of jobs.
2. Paragraph 2:
   a. The cotton mills of New England produced less cloth.
   b. Farms and businesses in the North had both successes and failures.
3. Paragraph 3:
   a. The South felt the effects of the war in several ways.
   b. Confederate money was almost useless.

money it became almost worthless. Study the two lists of prices below to see how the low value of money pushed prices up in the South.

Inflation in the South

	1860	1863
Bacon, 10 lbs.	$1.25	$10.00
Flour, 30 lbs.	1.50	3.75
Sugar, 5 lbs.	.40	5.75
Coffee, 4 lbs.	.50	20.00
Tea (green), ½ lb.	.50	8.00
Lard, 4 lbs.	.50	4.00
Butter, 3 lbs.	.75	5.25
Meal, 1 pkg.	.25	1.00
Candles, 2 lbs.	.30	2.50
Soap, 5 lbs.	.50	5.50
Total	$6.45	$65.75

The Letter Home, painting by Eastman Johnson

Southerners who lived nearest the war **zones** often suffered the most. In southern cities, the people faced shortages of wood, coal, clothing, and food. Available supplies went first to the military, then to civilians. Life in the country or on a farm was usually better, in that at least there was more food to eat. Still, goods such as salt and coffee were in short supply. Often the ground under a smoke house was dug up and sifted to find salt left over from salting the meat.

Civilians and the War

Washington and the Confederate capitals of Richmond and Montgomery buzzed with activity. Government workers swelled Washington's population. So did spies. Harriet Tubman, a former slave, was a spy for the North. A Maryland-born woman, Rose Greenhow, served as a spy for the South. She was so good at what she did that General George McClellan remarked bitterly, "She knew my plans and at four times compelled me to change them." Belle Boyd, another famous spy for the South, started her career at 17. By the age of 21, she was well-known in the North and had spent time in a northern prison.

In the capital cities, people also organized help for the soldiers. In past wars, soldiers often had endured cruel living conditions. Clara Barton, working for the North, organized aid for the soldiers—getting together clothing and scarce foods and bringing them herself to the battlefields. Her work provided a way for people on the home front to give direct aid to the war effort.

Before the Civil War, only men had been nurses. Working in Washington, Dorothea Dix organized women nurses for the North. Dr. Elizabeth Blackwell, America's first female doctor, became superintendent of nurses. In all, about 3,000 women served as nurses for the first time, in both the North and the South.

SECTION 4 REVIEW

1. How was each of the following affected by the Civil War: (a) northern farmers, (b) southern farmers, (c) northern industry owners, (d) southern city dwellers?
2. Which of the above groups do you think was hurt the most by the war? The least? Give reasons for your answer.
3. Give at least two examples of how prices changed in Richmond between 1860 and 1863. Why did prices change?
4. How did women's lives change during the war?

CLARA BARTON
(1821–1912)

During the Civil War, more soldiers died from disease and wound complications than were killed directly in battle. One person who worked to save lives was Clara Barton.

The youngest of five children, Barton was especially shy. When she was 15, her family pushed her into a teaching job in a nearby Massachusetts town in hopes of giving her self-confidence. She taught for the next 18 years, then became the first woman clerk in the U.S. Patent Office.

Living in Washington she heard many stories about the suffering of the wounded at the first battle of Bull Run. Doctors then did not know how germs carried diseases nor did they have medicines to kill germs. They often cut off the arms or legs of wounded soldiers to keep infection from spreading.

Barton decided to act to relieve the soldiers' suffering. At first, she spent her own money for medicines and supplies. Later she advertised for supplies in a newspaper. All during the war, she went to battles and gave out supplies and nursed the soldiers.

After the war, Barton went to Europe, where she again gave aid to the needy. Later, she founded the American Red Cross and served as its president from 1882 until 1904.

125

copperhead
emancipation
liberator

Abraham Lincoln, meeting with General George McClellan on the battlefield of Antietam, October 4, 1862

SECTION 5 Ending the War

Abraham Lincoln was President of the United States during the Civil War. Lincoln's job was difficult. He had to raise an army to fight a war that many northerners opposed. One group, called **copperheads**, encouraged Union soldiers to desert and smuggled military supplies to the South.

Fighting

One of Lincoln's biggest problems was that of finding a Union general who would "fight." Lincoln had, in fact, first asked Robert E. Lee to lead the Union forces, but when Virginia left the Union, Lee felt he had to be loyal to his state.

Lincoln first tried George B. McClellan, but he was slow and so overly cautious that Lincoln sent him this message: "If you are not going to use the army, then I would like to borrow it." Time after time, Lincoln replaced the Union commander—McClellan, Pope, Hooker, Burnside, McClellan, Meade. Finally, in March, 1864, Lincoln appointed Ulysses S. Grant to the job, and he found that he had his "fighting" general.

The North finally drove wedges through the South by capturing the Mississippi River in 1863 and Atlanta, Georgia, in September, 1864. After capturing Atlanta, the largest railroad center in Georgia, General William T. Sherman led his troops on a march through the state from Atlanta to Savannah. Sherman wanted southern civilians who supported the war to feel its impact. On the march to the sea, Sherman ordered his men to live off the land. In an area 300 miles long and 60 miles wide, his soldiers burned fields and barns, killed livestock, and destroyed bridges.

Sherman's victory at Atlanta and march to the sea left very bitter feelings in the South. However, it aided the Union cause in two ways. (1) It helped break the spirit of the South, and (2) it helped Lincoln win re-election in 1864.

Because of strong anti-war feelings, Lincoln faced a tough race for President. In the 1864 election, the Republicans renamed their party the Union party and asked a Tennessee Democrat, Andrew Johnson, to be their candidate for Vice-President. The Democrats nominated the former general George B. McClellan. With Sherman's victory in Atlanta, many northerners believed the war would soon end, and they elected Lincoln President and Johnson Vice-President.

Surrender

The North squeezed the South harder and harder. It tightened the blockade around southern ports, and fewer and fewer goods reached southern troops or people. Finally, the South was no longer able to fight. With his men practically starving, the Confederate general Robert E. Lee asked to meet with General Grant. On April 9, 1865, Lee surrendered to Grant in the village of Appomattox Court House, Virginia.

Grant was kind in his surrender terms. He allowed the southern soldiers to keep their horses, saying they would be needed for spring plowing. After the Union gave the southern soldiers much needed food, they returned to their homes. The war was over.

Freeing the Slaves

One of the biggest changes brought by the war was the freeing of the slaves. On January 1, 1863, Lincoln had issued the **Emancipation** Proclamation. It said that all slaves in the rebelling areas were free. It did not, however, free slaves in the border states or in territory already held by the Union. What it did do was to give the North a cause or reason for fighting the war—to free slaves. It also meant that as Union troops swept through the South, slaves greeted them as their **liberators**. The Emancipation Proclamation also helped keep England from aiding the South. Since the war was now

Defeated Confederate soldiers sadly furl their flag.

Lincoln's Death

Five days after the surrender at Appomattox, Lincoln went to a play at Ford's Theater in Washington, D.C. A southern fanatic, John Wilkes Booth, slipped up behind him and shot him in the head. Lincoln died the next day.

Lincoln's murder was part of a plot by a group of angry southerners to kill the top leaders in the Union. Although Secretary of State William Seward also was shot, he did not die from his wounds. The rest of the plot failed. Those who took part in the plot were tracked down, rapidly tried, and imprisoned or hanged for their part in killing the President.

being fought to free slaves, many abolitionists in England opposed giving aid to the South.

The actual freeing of all slaves in the United States was done through a constitutional amendment, Amendment 13. It was proposed by Congress in 1865 and ratified by three-quarters of the states that year. Amendment 14, granting citizenship to former slaves, was ratified in 1868. Two years later, Amendment 15, giving black males the right to vote, was ratified.

Other Results of the War

The cost of the Civil War was high. More Americans were killed and wounded in the Civil War than in any other American war, almost a million. The war was not only the bloodiest in the 1800s, it also cost more money than others in the century, some $15 billion, including property damages, which were mainly in the South.

Other results of the war were more positive. The Union was preserved, and the supremacy of the federal government established. The economic system of the "old South," based on plantations and slavery, was ended. Reconstruction, the process of bringing the South back into the Union, was begun.

The rest of the country also changed because of the war. Industry and business expanded and increased in the North. The West, too, began to develop. The Homestead Act, passed in 1862, gave free land to settlers. As a result, many white southerners and freed blacks moved westward after the war to start new lives.

SECTION 5 REVIEW

1. What was Lincoln searching for as he replaced General McClellan?
2. What was the Emancipation Proclamation? What did it do to help blacks?
3. What did Amendment 13 accomplish? Amendment 14? Amendment 15?
4. Give four results of the Civil War. Which do you think was the most important? Why?
5. What did the Homestead Act accomplish?
6. If your home had been in Georgia, how do you think you would have felt about northerners after General Sherman's march to the sea?

CHAPTER 22 ACTIVITIES

Wordpower!

Make up clues for each term in the crossword puzzle. Then use each in a sentence.

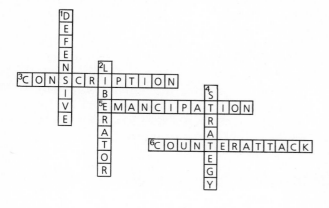

Across: 3.   5.   6.

Down: 1.   2.   4.

Reading Skills

Copy the following Section titles. Next to each write the phrase from the list below that best explains the subject of the section.

Section 1   Resources: North and South
Section 3   The Soldier's Life
Section 4   Life on the Home Front
Section 5   Ending the War

   a. existence between battles
   b. advantages and disadvantages
   c. the squeezing succeeds
   d. effects of war on city and farm

Writing Skills

From the table of battles on page 117, choose one for further study. Look in a book on the war and read carefully about that battle. Then write a newspaper story about the battle answering these questions: Who? What? Where? When? Why? How?

Figure It Out

At the beginning of the war both sides went off to war with high hopes. Their high spirits were reflected in their music. As the war dragged on, songs became slower and sadder. Read the two songs below, and decide which dates from the start of the war and which from the end. Support your decision by pointing to two phrases from each song that show either sadness or high spirits.

Somebody's Darling
(Popular with both sides)

Into the ward of the clean white-wash'd halls,
Where the dead slept and the dying lay;
Wounded by bayonets, sabres, and balls,
Somebody's darling was born one day.
Somebody's darling, so young and so brave.
Wearing still on his sweet, yet pale face,
Soon to be hid in the dust of the grave.
The lingering light of his boyhood's grace,
Somebody's darling, somebody's pride.
Who'll tell his mother where her boy died?

The Bonnie Blue Flag
(Next to "Dixie," the South's favorite marching song)

We are a band of brothers
And native to the soil
Fighting for our liberty
With treasure, blood and toil
And when our rights were threaten'd
The cry rose near and far,
Hurrah for the bonnie blue flag
That bears a single star!

Hurrah! Hurrah! For southern rights hurrah!
Hurrah for the bonnie blue flag
That bears a single star!

CHAPTER 23

Reconstruction

To **reconstruct** means to rebuild. The period after the Civil War is called **Reconstruction** because the rebuilding of the Union took place then. Reconstruction began in 1865, and most historians say it ended in 1877.

What really happened in the South during Reconstruction has been argued more by historians than the causes of the war. To some, Reconstruction was a disaster. To others it was a time of reform. In this chapter you will see why so many opinions are possible. Section 1 is about physical Reconstruction. Section 2 is about political Reconstruction. Section 3 describes the end of Reconstruction.

SECTION 1 Physical Reconstruction

The war officially ended on April 9, 1865, with Lee's surrender to Grant. The South lay in ruins, its cities shelled and its fields burnt by four years of war.

Most of the Union soldiers collected their pay, went home, and left the army. The southern soldiers went home, some walking hundreds of miles, without pay. Many had to beg for food as they traveled, and everywhere they looked, they saw the ruins of the South. The South had been defeated. Now how would it be rebuilt?

Finding Work

One thing had become certain as the war drew to a close: After the war, life in the South would *not* be based on slave labor and the plantation system. A planter who needed workers to plant and care for fields would have to hire them. A slave who had always lived on the same plantation and in the same cabin would have to find work and a home.

As slaves were freed, most left their former masters, even if they were offered jobs. Many freed slaves wandered for several months after the war ended, "breathing the air of freedom." However, large numbers returned to their home areas after several months and sought work. Those who returned to work for their former masters often felt that they had needed this time on their own to show that they were free.

A sketch, which appeared in an 1867 newspaper, shows a Union soldier reading freed slaves their rights.

(Left) April 1865, the burned ruins of Richmond, Virginia (Right) freed slaves at the end of the war, Richmond, Virginia

Chicago Historical Society

Most of the freed slaves had three goals: to find a job, to make a home, and to learn how to read and write. The freed slaves were soon able to marry and live in families without fear of being "sold down the river." As free people, they could own land, make contracts, and set up businesses.

The trouble was that although slaves could legally do all these things, few had any money to buy land or set up a business. Also, since the slave codes had outlawed teaching slaves to read and write, most former slaves were **illiterate**.

Government Help

In March, 1865, Congress set up the Bureau of Freedmen, Refugees, and Abandoned Lands, called the Freedmen's Bureau for short. The bureau gave food and clothing to homeless blacks and whites, set up schools, and tried to find homes for those whose lives had been torn apart in the war.

Back in 1863, there had been talk of giving every freed slave family "40 acres and a mule." Some leaders in Congress wanted to confiscate large plantations, divide the land into small plots, and give it to freed slaves. Congress decided any such action would go against the Constitution. Congress finally passed a law that let lands deserted by their owners be turned over to freed slaves. As a result, a few former slaves did get free land, although none got a free mule.

131

School for black children in Charleston, South Carolina, 1866

Reading Skills

Re-read the text listed below. To what do the following words refer?
1. Those (page 130, last paragraph)
   a. freed slaves
   b. months
   c. masters
2. They (page 131, line 4)
   a. white people
   b. families
   c. freed slaves
3. It (page 131, paragraph 4)
   a. Congress
   b. land
   c. a law
4. They (page 132, paragraph 3)
   a. workers
   b. planters
   c. fields

Within four years the Freedmen's Bureau had given out food and clothing to many blacks and whites. It set up 40 hospitals and settled almost 30,000 people into new homes. However, the Bureau's greatest success came in education. Under the Bureau's leadership, black colleges such as Howard University, Fisk University, Atlanta University, and Hampton Institute were founded. When the Bureau closed in 1870, about 250,000 blacks were in 4,300 schools in the South.

A New Way of Life

The Freedmen's Bureau helped, but most of the rebuilding of the South was done by the southern people themselves. Slowly, a new way of life grew up, based on a system of **sharecropping**.

Planters found that they did not have the money to hire workers to plant and care for their fields. All they owned was their land, and few people had money to buy land from them. So planters divided their land into plots and rented it to former slaves. Often, planters rented out tools and mules as well. Instead of paying a money rent, the former slaves paid the planters with a share of their crop. The freed slave lived in a cabin on the plot, grew some crops for food, and grew a "money crop," such as cotton or tobacco, to pay the rent.

Southern cities began to revive as trade centers as soon as the first crops were harvested in 1865. However, so many buildings, rail lines, bridges, and roads were destroyed in the war that it was many years before the South was rebuilt.

SECTION 1 REVIEW

1. What was the Freedmen's Bureau?
2. What was the greatest accomplishment of the Freedmen's Bureau?
3. Why didn't slave families get "40 acres and a mule"?
4. How did the system of sharecropping work?

SECTION 2 Political Reconstruction

Even before the war ended, Abraham Lincoln had presented his plan for reconstructing the Union. Under his plan, 10 percent of the number of voters in a state in the 1860 presidential election had to pledge their loyalty to the United States and agree to free their slaves. Then the state could elect members to Congress and act as if it had never tried to leave the Union. Only white men would vote, for while Lincoln opposed slavery, he had made no provisions for freed slaves to vote. Lincoln's "10 percent plan" was very lenient, or easy, on white southerners.

No one knows how well his plans would have worked, for six days after the war ended, Lincoln was assassinated. Vice-President Andrew Johnson became President.

Johnson was a Democrat from Tennessee and a firm supporter of the Union. He had owned slaves and was not anti-South, but he blamed the upper class of planters for starting the Civil War. He believed that they should be punished.

Johnson's Efforts

There was little difference between Johnson's plan for Reconstruction and Lincoln's. The biggest difference was that rich people had to ask the President for a pardon before they could take part in politics. This was Johnson's way of punishing the people he blamed for starting the war.

While Congress was not in session, most of the Confederate states met the requirements of the Johnson plan. They chose members of Congress and senators and began writing new state constitutions that outlawed slavery.

When Congress met in December, 1865, the Republicans and many northerners were outraged. The states reconstructed under Johnson's plan had elected many Confederate leaders to serve in Congress. The Vice-President of the Confederacy, four Confederate generals, six Confederate cabinet officers, and 58 members of the Confederate Congress had been elected to Congress. Also, former Confederates domi-

Glossary terms

black code
vagrancy
Radical Republicans

Reading Skills

To increase your skill at identifying word meanings by the underlined context, carefully read the sentences below. Then, locate a definition for each underlined word within its sentence. Copy the definition on your paper.
1. Lincoln's "10 percent plan" was very lenient, or easy, on white southerners.
2. Johnson blamed the planters, or upper class, in the South for starting the Civil War.
3. In 1868, Congress tried to impeach, or remove from office, Andrew Johnson.

133

ANDREW JOHNSON
(1808–1875)

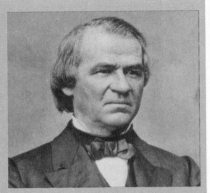

Andrew Johnson's life was a difficult one. His father died when he was two. His mother remarried and moved the family to Tennessee.

Apprenticed to a tailor at a young age, Johnson had no formal schooling. He did, however, have a strong desire to improve himself. He taught himself to be a good speaker by reading famous speeches.

In Tennessee, he helped form a workingman's party. Its members elected him to city office. From there, he moved up the ladder, by serving in Congress and as governor of Tennessee. He began serving in the Senate in 1857.

When the southern states voted to secede, their senators left Congress. Johnson did not. He stayed in the Senate and made several speeches in defense of the Union.

In 1864, although Johnson was a Democrat, the Republicans chose him to run as Vice-President so that they could claim to be a national party. The fact that he was not a Republican worked against him when Lincoln was assassinated.

Impeached by Congress in 1868, Johnson was found not guilty. After his term as President ended, he returned to Tennessee. In 1874, he was re-elected to the Senate.

nated the state and local governments of the South. Some of the same people who had led the war were now asking to be treated as if nothing had happened.

Angry northerners were shocked. Hadn't a war been fought and hundreds of thousands of northerners killed? Shouldn't the South be punished for starting the war?

Also, many southern states had passed **black codes** much like those that had governed slaves before the war. They restricted the movement of freed slaves. In some towns, blacks were not allowed into town without written permission from their employer. A black person who had no job could be arrested and fined for **vagrancy**. If he or she could not pay the fine, the person could be hired out to work for someone who could pay it. Blacks were also forbidden to testify against a white person in court.

To many northerners, the black codes seemed like an attempt to restore slavery. Even though many northern states had similar laws—about vagrancy, for example— Republicans in Congress were furious. They refused to seat the members of Congress from the South and set up their own harsher reconstruction plan.

Radical Reconstruction

The **Radical Republicans** were a group of men in Congress who thought the South should be punished for starting the war. Their leader in the Senate was Benjamin Wade. In the House, it was Thaddeus Stevens. In the congressional elections of 1866, Radical Republicans won control of Congress.

Led by the Radical Republicans, Congress passed the Military Reconstruction Act of 1867 over President Johnson's veto. The act divided the South into five military districts and put an army general in command of each. Federal troops were kept in the South to enforce the laws.

The generals were ordered to hold elections to choose delegates to state conventions that would write new state constitutions and set up new state governments. Only black men and those white men who had not taken part in the war could vote for delegates. When the state's voters had accepted the new state constitution, Congress would readmit the state into the Union.

Congress passed a number of other bills dealing with Reconstruction. They voted to keep the Freedmen's Bureau alive, for example. Johnson also opposed and vetoed these laws, but his vetos were overridden by Congress.

Even before the war ended, Congress had proposed Amendment 13 to the United States Constitution, which ended slavery. It was ratified by three-fourths of the states in 1865. In order to protect the rights of freed slaves, the Radical Republicans proposed two more amendments. Amendment 14 guaranteed citizenship to blacks. Amendment 15 gave black men the right to vote. Congress required the southern states to ratify Amendment 14 in order to be readmitted to the Union.

Johnson vs. Congress

President Andrew Johnson and the Congress did not agree about many of the plans for Reconstruction. As time passed, strong hatred began to brew. Congress tried to block the President from acting, and the President tried to block Congress.

In 1867, Congress passed the Tenure of Office Act. This law said the President could not remove any Cabinet member without the permission of Congress. The law was passed to protect Secretary of War Edwin Stanton, a supporter of the Radical Republicans.

For another year, Congress and Johnson played cat and mouse. Then, in February, 1868, irritated by Stanton's disloyalty to him, Johnson fired the Secretary of War. Johnson's enemies pounced. The House of Representatives voted to impeach Johnson for breaking a law passed by Congress. Chief Justice Samuel Chase presided over the trial in the Senate.

At first, many northerners favored finding Johnson guilty and removing him from office. As the trial dragged through April and May, they began to change their minds. The Radical Republicans had based their testimony on emotional issues. One Republican, Benjamin Butler, even waved a nightshirt supposedly stained with the blood of a northerner who had been beaten in the South. (For years after, "waving the bloody shirt" was a saying used to refer to the practice of reminding Americans that the South had started the war.)

Johnson's lawyers, on the other hand, were very professional. They pointed out that the Tenure of Office Act was clearly unconstitutional. When the vote was taken, the result was *one* vote short of the number needed to remove Johnson from office. Still, although Johnson was not removed from office, he was a beaten man. He had lost political support.

In the election of 1868, the Republicans nominated war hero Ulysses S. Grant for President. The Democrats chose Horatio Seymour. Grant easily won.

SUSAN B. ANTHONY
(1820–1906)

During the Civil War, reformers who worked for women's rights moved out of the spotlight. Fighting the war and ending slavery became the main goals of reformers. One person who helped move women back into the spotlight was Susan B. Anthony.

A Quaker, Anthony was encouraged by her parents to think and to be self-supporting. In 1851, she met Elizabeth Cady Stanton. Together they formed a strong team, working to win legal rights for women. Often met with boos, hisses, rotten eggs, and tomatoes, they continued to speak out.

Many women's rights groups also worked for the freedom of the slaves. After the Civil War, Anthony and her followers tried to win for women the same rights as freed slaves.

The result was a split in the women's rights movement. Frederick Douglass and other abolitionists who had supported women's rights, declared this time in history to be the "Negro's hour." They thought women should wait.

In 1869, Anthony and Stanton formed the National Woman Suffrage Association. From then until the 1890s, it was the major group working to win women the right to vote.

135

1. What did Lincoln's "10 percent plan" require the southern states to do?
2. How did Johnson become President?
3. In what ways did Johnson's Reconstruction plan differ from Lincoln's?
4. Why did the Radical Republicans feel that the South deserved a harsher Reconstruction plan?
5. Explain the Reconstruction plan passed by Congress in 1867.
6. How was the Tenure of Office Act used against President Johnson?

Glossary terms

scalawag
carpetbagger
terrorist
white supremacy

Anti-carpetbagger cartoon by Thomas Nast, 1872

SECTION 3 The End of Reconstruction

Political Reconstruction officially came to an end when the last federal troops were removed from Louisiana and South Carolina in 1877. However, in some states, it ended by 1870.

Violence in the South

Many white people resented the idea that black people were equal to them politically and legally. Some even turned to violence. They singled out three groups for attack—black leaders, **scalawags**, and **carpetbaggers**.

Black leaders. With freedom, some black men became political leaders in the South. Black men made up 10 to 61 percent of the new state legislatures, but none was elected governor. Sixteen black men were elected to the U.S. House of Representatives and two black men to the U.S. Senate.

A look at the two men elected to the Senate reveals what these leaders were like. Hiram Revels and Blanche K. Bruce both represented Mississippi in the Senate. They were well educated, successful, and well liked.

Revels had been born a free black in North Carolina. He studied at Knox College in Illinois and then moved to Maryland. There he became a teacher and a minister of the African Methodist Episcopal Church. During the war, Revels recruited blacks for the Union army and founded a school for former slaves in St. Louis, Missouri. At the end of the war he moved to Natchez, Mississippi, where he became involved in politics. In 1870, he was elected to the Senate.

Blanche K. Bruce had been born a slave in Viriginia. He escaped to Missouri during the war and began teaching school. Bruce moved to Mississippi after the war and became a wealthy planter. He entered politics and served in a number of posts before being elected to the Senate in 1874.

The kind of leadership black men gave was similar to that given by whites. Some did a good job, some a bad job, and some a job that was in-between. However, no matter how good a job they did, they could not please many whites. Resentful white people tried to find ways to take away the political power of newly freed black people.

Almost all black political leaders were Republicans. For that reason, white groups tried to keep blacks from voting for the Republican party. Black men might be told that if they wanted to keep their jobs, they had better vote Democratic. Black Republicans who did show up to vote might face armed whites at the polling place. Merely urging other blacks to vote Republican was a way to invite attack.

Scalawags and carpetbaggers. Scalawags were white southerners who had joined with the Republicans in the South. Other white southerners often viewed them as low-lifes that had crawled out from under a rock. Although some scalawags had become Republicans to get ahead, others were well-to-do, upper-class whites who wanted to help the South peacefully. Among the scalawags was the former governor of Georgia, Joseph Brown, who had seen enough of violence in the war.

Carpetbaggers were white northerners who settled in the South after the war. Because some carried suitcases made of carpet, all migrating northerners were called carpetbaggers. Some were people who came to make money off the war-torn South, but many had come to help the freed slaves and to help rebuild the South.

Terrorists. Some white southerners formed terrorist groups to attack blacks, scalawags, and carpetbaggers. For example, realizing that education was the key to black advancement, they burned or tore down schools. They threatened, beat, ran out of town, and even murdered teachers.

The Ku Klux Klan became the best-known **terrorist** group. Organized in Tennessee in 1865, the Klan moved throughout the South to restore what its members called "law and order." In the spring of 1867, delegates met at a Klan convention in Nashville, Tennessee, and chose the former Confederate general Nathan B. Forrest to lead them.

By using terror to stop blacks from voting or exercising other rights, the Klan worked to re-establish **white supremacy** in the South. Other groups, such as the Knights of the Rising Sun and the White Line, also formed groups to oppose black equality.

BLANCHE K. BRUCE
(1841–1898)

Blanche K. Bruce was the first black American to serve a full term in the Senate. Born a slave in Virginia, he was taught how to read and write by his white half-brother. In 1861, he escaped to Missouri. There he taught school and began to show the leadership that would one day lead him to the Senate.

After the Civil War, he attended Oberlin College in Ohio for two years, then moved to Mississippi. He became a wealthy planter and began to work in politics. His honesty gained him much respect and led to his election to the Senate.

While Bruce served in the Senate from 1875 until 1881, he was very much concerned about the problems of former slaves. He also worked for fair treatment for American Indians and for Chinese immigrants.

Although Reconstruction was a period of graft and corruption, none of it touched Bruce. He worked hard to represent his state and its people.

With the end of Reconstruction, it became impossible for him to be re-elected to the Senate. However, he was appointed to various positions in the government. He was Register of the Treasury at the time of his death.

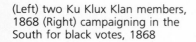
(Left) two Ku Klux Klan members, 1868 (Right) campaigning in the South for black votes, 1868

Response to Terror

When terrorist attacks began, Congress passed laws and used soldiers to end violence. However, after 1868, the Radical Republicans slowly lost control of Congress. Also, northerners lost their appetite for trying to force white southerners to treat freed slaves as equals. There were several reasons.

First, with the death of Thaddeus Stevens in 1868, the Radical Republicans lost their strongest leader. No other white leader appeared who felt as strongly about the rights of black people.

Second, many northerners had tired of the Civil War and Reconstruction. By 1870, all of the southern states had been readmitted to Congress. Northerners became far more concerned with their own problems.

Third, many white northerners feared competition from black workers. They did not want to do anything that would encourage competition from blacks.

Fourth, Grant's two terms as President were so corrupt they gave the Republicans a bad name in the North as well as among white southerners. In the congressional elections of

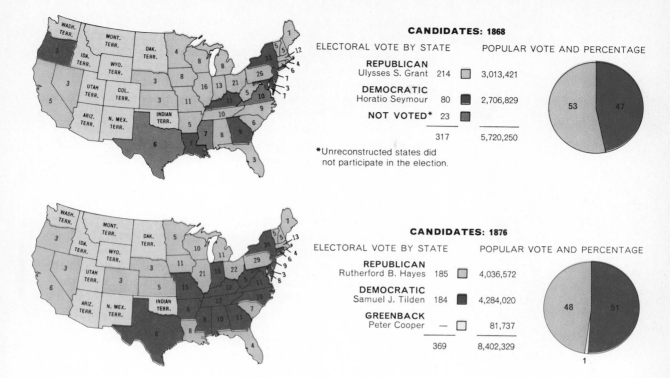

CANDIDATES: 1868

ELECTORAL VOTE BY STATE | POPULAR VOTE AND PERCENTAGE

REPUBLICAN
Ulysses S. Grant 214 ☐ 3,013,421

DEMOCRATIC
Horatio Seymour 80 ■ 2,706,829

NOT VOTED* 23 ■

317 5,720,250

*Unreconstructed states did
not participate in the election.

CANDIDATES: 1876

ELECTORAL VOTE BY STATE | POPULAR VOTE AND PERCENTAGE

REPUBLICAN
Rutherford B. Hayes 185 ☐ 4,036,572

DEMOCRATIC
Samuel J. Tilden 184 ■ 4,284,020

GREENBACK
Peter Cooper — ☐ 81,737

369 8,402,329

1874, Democrats won control of the House of Representatives for the first time since the election of 1856. All of these reasons helped lead to the end of Reconstruction.

Election of 1876

The end to political Reconstruction came about through one of the strangest elections in American history—the presidential election of 1876. The Republicans nominated Rutherford B. Hayes for President. The Democrats chose Samuel J. Tilden.

Tilden received a clear majority of the popular votes and appeared to have been elected President. However, the electoral votes from Oregon, Florida, South Carolina, and Louisiana were disputed. Both Democrats and Republicans claimed them. Without the votes of these states, Tilden had 184 electoral votes—one less than the number then needed for election.

Normally, if no candidate has a majority of the electoral votes, the House of Representatives chooses the President. The problem in this election was that both candidates

What happened to the number of popular votes and electoral votes between 1868 and 1876? On the basis of electoral votes, which candidate should have won the election of 1876? Which candidate won the majority of popular votes? Which candidate was finally declared elected and under what circumstances?

claimed to have a majority of the electoral votes. Tilden's backers said that he had clearly won the election in Florida and Louisiana and should receive the votes of those states (giving Tilden a total of 196 electoral votes). Hayes' backers claimed that their candidate had won all four disputed states. With the votes of the four states, Hayes had 185 electoral votes, the number needed to become President.

To settle the dispute, Congress appointed a committee of five House members, five senators, and five members of the Supreme Court. The committee included eight Republicans and seven Democrats, and it gave all of the disputed votes to Hayes, making him President.

Many Democrats were so angry with the results that they threatened to stop the inauguration of Hayes. Finally, a compromise was reached. (1) Hayes became President. (2) Hayes agreed to remove all remaining federal troops from the South. (3) The Republicans promised federal aid to help the South's economy mostly by rebuilding railroads. With the Compromise of 1877, the Democrats regained control in the South and political Reconstruction ended.

Results of Reconstruction

Probably the greatest results of Reconstruction were Amendments 13, 14, and 15. They abolished slavery, defined citizenship, and gave black men the right to vote. Other gains included public schools and the abolition of property requirements for voting.

However, most white southerners never accepted blacks as their equals. Many did all they could to keep blacks from using their newly won rights. For example, white politicians found many ways to keep blacks from voting.

Bitter feelings were another result. For years, many white southerners associated Reconstruction with Republicans and refused to vote Republican. The South became a solid Democratic stronghold. State officials and members of Congress were always members of the Democratic party. Until the 1950s, Republicans rarely won an election in the South.

Reading Skills

This section deals with causes and effects. Re-read each passage listed and decide if it is mostly about causes or effects.
1. Page 136, paragraph 1, beginning "Political Reconstruction officially came to an end. . . ."
2. Page 138, paragraph 3, beginning "Second, many northerners. . . ."
3. Page 138, paragraph 4, beginning "Third, many white northerners. . . ."
4. Page 140, paragraph 5, beginning, "Probably the greatest. . . ."

SECTION 3 REVIEW

1. What were scalawags and carpetbaggers?
2. How did terrorist groups prevent blacks from voting?
3. Why did Reconstruction end in the South?
4. Explain three results of Reconstruction.
5. Why was the presidential election of 1876 disputed?

CHAPTER 23 ACTIVITIES

Wordpower!

Unscramble each term in capital letters to spell out a term from the chapter.

1. The Ku Klux Klan and other ORTERISTR groups worked to keep freed slaves from voting.
2. A northerner who had settled in the South after the war was called a GERBAGPETCAR.
3. A southerner who helped Republicans in the South was called a LAASCGAW.
4. In the period of TIONSTRUCRECON, the South was returned to the Union.

Reading Skills

Which outline below correctly shows the organization of this chapter?

1. a. Changing laws
   b. Rebuilding ruins
   c. Closing an era
2. a. Rebuilding ruins
   b. Johnson's plan
   c. Closing an era
3. a. Rebuilding ruins
   b. Changing laws
   c. Closing an era

Figure It Out

Abraham Lincoln visited Gettysburg, Pennsylvania, in November, 1863, to dedicate a cemetery for several thousand soldiers who had died in battle there that July. Lincoln made the speech that follows, which became one of the most famous speeches in American history.

After you read this speech, answer the following questions:

1. Why do you think Lincoln gave this speech?
2. Why did Lincoln believe the soldiers at Gettysburg had not died in vain?
3. Was Lincoln speaking of northern soldiers, southern soldiers, or both? Give evidence to support your answer.

4. What ideas in the speech might apply to the problems of today?

"Four score and seven years ago our fathers brought forth on this continent a new nation, conceived in liberty and dedicated to the proposition that all men are created equal.

Now we are engaged in a great civil war, testing whether that nation or any nation, so conceived and so dedicated can long endure. We are met on a great battlefield of that war. We have come to dedicate a portion of that field as a final resting place for those who here gave their lives that that nation might live. It is altogether fitting and proper that we should do this.

But in a larger sense, we cannot dedicate—we cannot consecrate—we cannot hallow—this ground. The brave men, living and dead, who struggled here, have consecrated it far above our poor power to add or detract. The world will little note, nor long remember what we say here, but it can never forget what they did here. It is for us the living, rather, to be dedicated here to the unfinished work which they who fought here have thus far so nobly advanced.

It is rather for us to be here dedicated to the great task remaining before us—that from these honored dead we take increased devotion to that cause for which they gave the last full measure of devotion—that we here highly resolve that these dead shall not have died in vain—that this nation, under God, shall have a new birth of freedom—and that government of the people, by the people, for the people, shall not perish from the earth."

Writing Skills

Was Reconstruction a disaster or a time of reform? State your views in a one-paragraph essay. Give three or four reasons for your opinion, using the material in the chapter as evidence.

UNIT 8 TEST

In your notebook, write the answers to the following questions.

Completion
In each blank, write the term that best completes the sentence.

terrorist   defensive
counterattack   conscription
illiterate   liberators
Radical   deserted

1. The Confederate strategy was based on fighting a _____ war.
2. The Confederates stopped retreating at Manassas, and "Stonewall" Jackson led their _____ on the Union forces.
3. Both the North and the South passed _____ laws to draft white men into the army.
4. Some soldiers _____ and went home to their families.
5. The Emancipation Proclamation led southern slaves to view the Union forces as their _____.
6. Because slave codes outlawed teaching slaves to read and write, most slaves were _____.
7. The _____ Republicans in Congress forced a harsh Reconstruction plan on the South.
8. A _____ group is a secret group that uses violence to frighten other people.

Multiple Choice
Choose the ending that best completes each sentence.
1. The first shot of the Civil War was fired at:
   a. Bull Run
   b. Fort Sumter
   c. Manassas
2. The leading Confederate general was:
   a. Robert E. Lee
   b. George B. McClellan
   c. Ulysses S. Grant
3. The leading Union general was:
   a. Robert E. Lee
   b. "Stonewall" Jackson
   c. Ulysses S. Grant
4. The Emancipation Proclamation:
   a. freed all the slaves
   b. freed the slaves in the Confederacy
   c. freed slaves in Washington, D.C.
5. Sherman's march to the sea:
   a. broke the spirit of the North
   b. made Sherman popular in Georgia
   c. broke the spirit of the South
6. When Lincoln was shot, the Vice-President of the United States was:
   a. George McClellan   c. Jefferson Davis
   b. Andrew Johnson
7. The organization formed in March, 1865, to aid newly freed slaves was the:
   a. Carpetbagger Society c. Ku Klux Klan
   b. Freedmen's Bureau
8. The laws passed by the southern states after the war that restricted the rights of former slaves were:
   a. Amendments 13, 14, and 15
   b. slave codes   c. black codes
9. The law that divided the South into five military districts and abolished all state governments was:
   a. Amendment 13   b. the Tenure of Office Act
   c. the Military Reconstruction Act of 1867
10. Black men gained the right to vote through:
    a. the 13th Amendment
    b. the 14th Amendment
    c. the 15th Amendment
11. The amendment that abolished slavery was:
    a. the 13th Amendment
    b. the 14th Amendment
    c. the 15th Amendment
12. A group that used terror against blacks, was:
    a. the Knights of Columbia
    b. the Knights of Labor
    c. the Ku Klux Klan

Reading Graphic Aids

The period of Reconstruction has often been called a time of "black rule." Critics of blacks claimed that freed slaves controlled the governments of the South.

Study the following chart, which shows the make-up of the state conventions elected when military leaders ran the elections.

1. In which state were a majority of the delegates black Americans?
2. In which states were most of the delegates white southerners?
3. Which of the following statements best describes the chart? Give reasons for your answer.
   a. Whites outnumbered blacks almost 3–1 in the state conventions.
   b. Blacks were an important force in three states.
   c. White northerners made up a bigger percentage of the delegates in more states than did blacks.
   d. White southerners controlled all but four state conventions.

Tricky Questions

If a statement is true, write "T" next to it. If it is false, correct it to make it true.

1. Southerners had the advantage of fighting a defensive war on their own land.
2. At the start of the war, the North had the best military leaders.
3. The turning point of the war came in 1864.
4. Life for a soldier was usually exciting and fun.
5. Soldiers usually cooked their own food over an open fire.
6. Most of the soldiers were about 35.
7. The Emancipation Proclamation freed all of the slaves in the United States.
8. Amendment 14 freed slaves and gave black men the right to vote.

Essay

American life and politics underwent many important changes after the Civil War. In a one-paragraph essay, explain three or four of these changes. Put them in order of their importance, ending with the one you believe the most important.

Membership of State Conventions 1867–1868

State	Black	White Native	White Northern	Total	Total Number	Black	White Native	White Northern
Alabama	18	59	31	90	108	17	55	28
Arkansas	8	35	23	58	66	13	52	35
Florida	18	12	15	27	45	40	27	33
Georgia	33	128	9	137	170	19	74	7
Louisiana	49	*	*	49	98	50	*	*
Mississippi	17	29	54	83	100	17	29	54
North Carolina	15	100	18	118	133	11	75	14
South Carolina	76	27	21	48	124	61	22	17
Virginia	25	33	47	80	105	24	31	45
Texas	9	*	*	81	90	10	*	*
Total	268	423	218	771				

*Further breakdown unavailable.

ARCTIC OCEAN

80°N

180°

160°W

140°West Longitude

80°W

Greenl
(DENMA

Arctic Circle

Alaska
(U.S.)

60°N

CANADA

**NORTH
AMERICA**

ATLANT
OCEAN

Aleutian Islands

40°North Latitude

UNITED STATES

Azores
(PORT.)

**PACIFIC
OCEAN**

Midway Islands
(U.S.)

Bermuda
(U.K.)

Tropic of Cancer

Hawaii (U.S.)

MEXICO

CUBA

BAHAMAS

DOMINICAN
REPUBLIC

Puerto Rico (U.S.)

20°N

JAMAICA

HAITI

ANTIGUA-BARBUDA
DOMINICA

CAPE VE

BELIZE

Virgin Is. (U.S.-U.K.)

ST. LUCIA

ST. VINCENT AND
THE GRENADINES

GUATEMALA

HONDURAS

EL SALVADOR

NICARAGUA

GRENADA

BARBADOS

TRINIDAD AND TOBAGO

COSTA RICA

VENEZUELA

GUYANA

PANAMA

SURINAME

KIRIBATI

COLOMBIA

FR. GUIANA
(FRANCE)

0°

Equator

ECUADOR

Galapagos
Islands
(ECUADOR)

**SOUTH
AMERICA**

P O L Y N E S I A

PERU

WESTERN
SAMOA

American
Samoa (U.S.)

BRAZIL

TONGA

French
Polynesia
(FRANCE)

BOLIVIA

20°S

PARAGUAY

Tropic of Capricorn

Easter Island
(CHILE)

CHILE

URUGUAY

ARGENTINA

40°S

**PACIFIC
OCEAN**

Falkland Islands
(U.K.)

South Georgia
(Falkland Is.)

60°S

Antarctic Circle

80°S

ANTARCTICA

180°

160°W

140°W

120°W

100°W

80°W

60

EUROPE

60°N

10°W

0°

NORWAY

SWEDEN

IRELAND

UNITED
KINGDOM

DENMARK

50°N

NETHERLANDS

EAST
GERMANY

POLAND

BELGIUM

WEST
GERMANY

CZECHOSLOVAKIA

U.S.S.R.

LUX.

**ATLANTIC
OCEAN**

FRANCE

AUSTRIA

HUNGARY

SWITZERLAND

ROMANIA

YUGOSLAVIA

ITALY

BULGARIA

PORTUGAL

SPAIN

ALBANIA

GREECE

20°E

500 Miles

0

0

500 Kilometers

MALTA

CYPRUS

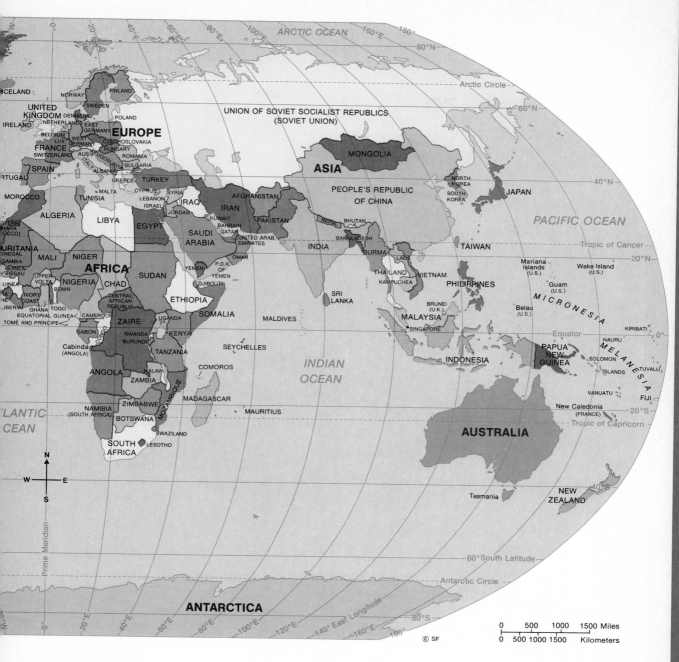

ARCTIC OCEAN

Arctic Circle

ICELAND

NORWAY
SWEDEN
FINLAND

UNITED
KINGDOM
DENMARK
POLAND

IRELAND

NETHERLANDS
EAST
GERMANY

BELGIUM
WEST
GERMANY

LUX.
CZECHOSLOVAKIA

EUROPE

UNION OF SOVIET SOCIALIST REPUBLICS
(SOVIET UNION)

60°N

FRANCE
SWITZERLAND
AUS.
HUNGARY

ROMANIA

PORTUGAL
SPAIN
ITALY
YUGOS.
BULGARIA

ALBANIA
GREECE
TURKEY

ASIA

MONGOLIA

40°N

NORTH
KOREA

SOUTH
KOREA

JAPAN

MALTA
CYPRUS
SYRIA

MOROCCO
TUNISIA
LEBANON
ISRAEL
JORDAN
IRAQ

IRAN

AFGHANISTAN

PEOPLE'S REPUBLIC
OF CHINA

ALGERIA
LIBYA
EGYPT
KUWAIT
BAHRAIN
QATAR

PAKISTAN

NEPAL
BHUTAN

PACIFIC OCEAN

WESTERN
SAHARA
(MOROCCO)

SAUDI
ARABIA

UNITED ARAB
EMIRATES

BANGLADESH

TAIWAN

Tropic of Cancer

MAURITANIA

MALI
NIGER

SENEGAL
GAMBIA
GUINEA-
BISSAU

AFRICA

SUDAN

OMAN

INDIA

BURMA

LAOS

Mariana
Islands
(U.S.)

Wake Island
(U.S.)

20°N

P.D.R.
OF
YEMEN

THAILAND
VIETNAM

Guam
(U.S.)

MICRONESIA

GUINEA
UPPER
VOLTA
NIGERIA
CHAD
YEMEN
DJIBOUTI
KAMPUCHEA

SIERRA
LEONE
IVORY
COAST
GHANA
TOGO
BENIN

CENTRAL
AFRICAN
REPUBLIC

ETHIOPIA

SRI
LANKA

PHILIPPINES

Belau
(U.S.)

LIBERIA

EQUATORIAL GUINEA
CAMEROON

SOMALIA

BRUNEI
(U.K.)

SÃO TOMÉ AND PRÍNCIPE

ZAIRE
UGANDA
KENYA

MALDIVES

MALAYSIA

KIRIBATI

NAURU

0°

GABON
CONGO
RWANDA
BURUNDI

SINGAPORE

Equator

MELANESIA

Cabinda
(ANGOLA)

TANZANIA

SEYCHELLES

**INDIAN
OCEAN**

INDONESIA

PAPUA
NEW
GUINEA

SOLOMON
ISLANDS

TUVALU

ANGOLA

MALAWI

ZAMBIA

COMOROS

VANUATU

FIJI

MOZAMBIQUE

MADAGASCAR

**ATLANTIC
OCEAN**

NAMIBIA
(SOUTH AFRICA)

ZIMBABWE

BOTSWANA

MAURITIUS

New Caledonia
(FRANCE)

20°S

Tropic of Capricorn

SWAZILAND

AUSTRALIA

SOUTH
AFRICA
LESOTHO

N

W E

S

40°S

Tasmania

**NEW
ZEALAND**

Prime Meridian

60°South Latitude

Antarctic Circle

ANTARCTICA

0   500   1000   1500 Miles

© SF

0   500 1000 1500   Kilometers

AUS.—AUSTRIA
LUX.—LUXEMBOURG
P.D.R. OF YEMEN—PEOPLE'S DEMOCRATIC REPUBLIC OF YEMEN
PORT.—PORTUGAL
U.K.—UNITED KINGDOM (BRITAIN)
U.S.—UNITED STATES
U.S.S.R.—UNION OF SOVIET SOCIALIST REPUBLICS

United States—Political, Physical, and Elevation

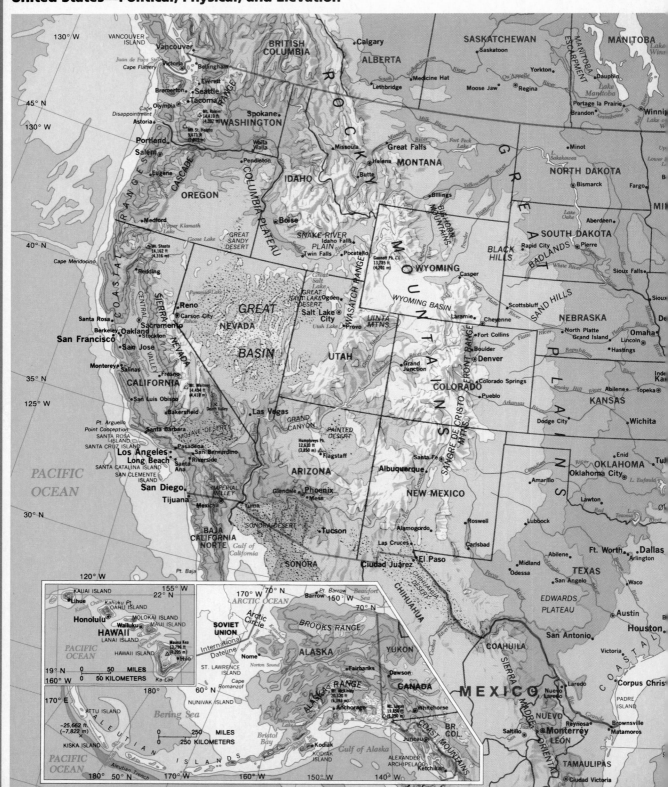

CANADA
CANADIAN SHIELD
HUDSON BAY LOWLANDS
James Bay
Hudson Bay Lowlands
80° W
50° N
Port-Cartier
NEWFOUNDLAND
ANTICOSTI ISLAND
Cape Gaspé
Gulf of St. Lawrence
ST. PIERRE & MIQUELON (FR.)
Moosonee
LAURENTIAN HIGHLANDS
Baie-Comeau
Rimouski
GASPÉ PEN.
Gaspé
MAGDALEN ISLAND
Cabot Strait
Kapuskasing
QUEBEC
Chicoutimi
NOTRE DAME MTNS.
Bathurst
PRINCE EDWARD ISLAND
Glace Bay
Sydney
Cape Breton
45° N
ONTARIO
John Saguenay R.
Rivière-du-Loup
Chatham
NEW BRUNSWICK
Charlottetown
CAPE BRETON I.
Timmins
Rouyn
Val-d'Or
Couin Reservoir
Edmunston
Moncton
New Glasgow
Kirkland Lake
Cabonga Reservoir
St. John
Fredericton
Truro
Cambridge
Lake Nipigon
Sudbury
LAURENTIAN SCARP
Trois Rivières
Thetford Mines
MAINE
Dartmouth
Halifax
NOVA SCOTIA
ISLE ROYALE
UPLAND
Lake Superior
Sault Ste. Marie
North Bay
Ottawa
Cornwall
Montreal
Laval
Sherbrooke
Quebec
Bangor
Augusta
Cape Sable
nder Bay
Marquette
MANITOULIN ISLAND
Mt. Washington 6,288 ft. (1,916 m)
Lewiston
Bay of Fundy
Peterborough
Kingston
ADIRONDACK MTNS.
VT.
Concord
N.H.
Portsmouth
Portland
Lake Huron
Toronto
Oshawa
Montpelier
Burlington
Lake Champlain
Manchester
WISCONSIN
Wausau
Green Bay
Oshkosh
MICHIGAN
Hamilton
St. Catharines
Niagara Falls
Lake Ontario
Rochester
Syracuse
Utica
Schenectady
Albany
NEW YORK
Worcester
Boston
MASS.
Cape Cod
Lake Michigan
Saginaw
Kitchener
Niagara
Buffalo
ALLEGHENY PLATEAU
Springfield
Hartford
Providence
R.I.
NANTUCKET ISLAND
MARTHA'S VINEYARD
60° W
40° N
Madison
Milwaukee
Racine
Sheboygan
Lake Winnebago
Grand Rapids
Flint
London
Sarnia
Chatham
CONN.
New Haven
ATLANTIC OCEAN
Rockford
Kalamazoo
Lansing
Detroit
Windsor
Lake Erie
Scranton
Paterson
Yonkers
LONG ISLAND
Chicago
Gary
Hammond
South Bend
Ft. Wayne
Akron
Cleveland
PENNSYLVANIA
Newark
New York City
New York
N.J.
Joliet
Peoria
CENTRAL
INDIANA
Lima
OHIO
Youngstown
Harrisburg
Allentown
Reading
Trenton
Philadelphia
Camden
Atlantic City
Waukegan
Muncie
Columbus
Pittsburgh
Altoona
Wheeling
APPALACHIAN MOUNTAINS
Wilmington
Baltimore
ILLINOIS
LOWLANDS
Champaign
Indianapolis
Dayton
Cincinnati
Parkersburg
Hagerstown
MD.
Bethesda
Dover
Cape May
DEL.
Delaware Bay
Springfield
WEST VIRGINIA
Charleston
VIRGINIA
Arlington
Annapolis
Washington D.C.
St. Louis
East St. Louis
Terre Haute
Evansville
Frankfort
Louisville
Lexington
Huntington
Charlottesville
Richmond
Cape Charles
KENTUCKY
BLUE RIDGE MTNS.
Roanoke
Newport News
Hampton
Portsmouth
Norfolk
Dismal Swamp
Albemarle Sound
CUMBERLAND PLATEAU
Greensboro
HATTERAS ISLAND
Cape Hatteras
Nashville
Knoxville
Mt. Mitchell 6,684 ft. (2,037 m)
Winston-Salem
Raleigh
PIEDMONT
Memphis
Chattanooga
Asheville
APPALACHIAN
NORTH CAROLINA
Charlotte
Huntsville
TENNESSEE
SOUTH CAROLINA
Wilmington
Cape Fear
COASTAL PLAIN
Athens
Columbia
Bluff
Birmingham
Tuscaloosa
Atlanta
Macon
Charleston
Greenville
ALABAMA
GEORGIA
Columbus
Savannah
MISSISSIPPI
Jackson
Montgomery
Meridian
Okefenokee Swamp
Baton Rouge
Biloxi
Pensacola
Mobile
Jacksonville
ew Orleans
Gulfport
Mobile Bay
Tallahassee
St. Augustine
ayette
Breton Sound
Apalachee Bay
FLORIDA
Daytona Beach
Cape San Blas
Waccasassa Bay
Ocala
Orlando
Cape Canaveral
Gulf of Mexico
St. Petersburg
Tampa
Tampa Bay
Sarasota
GRAND BAHAMA
GREAT ABACO
Lake Okeechobee
Ft. Lauderdale
Miami
Miami Beach
BAHAMAS
ELEUTHERA
Cape Sable
The Everglades
Nassau
CAT
70° W
Key West
FLORIDA KEYS
Straits of Florida
75° W
20° N
Cancer
90° W
85° W
80° W
Havana
CUBA

Feet (Meters)
10,000 (3,000)
7,000 (2,000)
3,000 (1,000)
1,500 (500)
700 (200)
0 (0): Sea Level
Below Sea Level
700 (200)
10,000 (3,000)
20,000 (6,000)
Deeper than 20,000

Deserts
Land under ice
International boundaries
State or provincial boundaries
★ National capitals
◉ State or provincial capitals
• Other cities

0   125   250 MILES
0   125   250 KILOMETERS

N
W — E
S

ATLAS

© SF

GLOSSARY

Key

hat, āge, fär; let, ēqual, tėrm; it,
īce; hot, ōpen, ôrder; oil, out;
cup, pùt, rüle;

ə represents *a* in about, *e* in taken, *i*
in pencil, *o* in lemon, *u* in circus.

abbreviations: *adj.* is *adjective*, *adv.*
is *adverb*, *n.* is *noun*, *pl.* is *plural*,
sing. is *singular*, *v.i.* is *intransitive
verb*, *v.t.* is *transitive verb*.

a bol ish (ə bol'ish), *v.t.* do away with completely,
261.

ab o li tion ist (ab'ə lish'ə nist), *n.* person who
favored the compulsory ending of slavery in
the United States, 215.

al ter na tive (ôl ter'nə tiv), *n.* choice from among
two or more things, 261.

an nex (ə neks'), *v.t.* join or add to a larger or more
important thing, 256.

balance of power distribution of power so that one
faction does not become strong enough to
dominate or conquer the other, 265–266.

black code law passed in some southern states
after the Civil War limiting the rights of the
freed slaves, 306.

block ade (blo kād'), *n.* a blocking of a place by
military means, especially with ships, to control who or what goes into or out of it, 183,
634.

cap i tal (kap'ə təl), *n.* money put to a productive
use, such as building roads, railroads, farms,
plantations, and businesses, 231.

car pet bag ger (kär'pit bag'ər), *n.* a white northerner who settled in the South after the Civil
War, so called because many of the migrating
northerners carried everything they owned in a
bag made of carpet, 308, 309.

cau cus (kô kəs), *n.* a meeting of members or leaders of a political party to make plans, choose
candidates, or decide how to vote, 209–210.

civil war war between opposing groups of one
nation, 269.

Con fed er a cy (kən fed'ər ə sē), *n.* a group of eleven southern states that seceded from the
Union in 1860 and 1861, and formed a new
government for the South called the Confederate States of America, 275.

con fis cate (kon'fə skāt), *v.t.*, -**cated**, -**cating**. seize
for the public treasury; seize by authority, 275.

con scrip tion (kən skrip'shən), *n.* compulsory service of men in the armed forces, 291.

con se quence (kon'sə kwens), *n.* result or effect,
261.

cop per head (kop'ər hed'), *n.* a northerner who
favored the South during the Civil War, 298.

cor po ra tion (kôr pə rā'shən), *n.* a group of persons given the power to carry on a business,
with authority to act as a single person, 231.

cor rupt (kə rupt'), *adj.* morally bad; influenced by
bribes; dishonest, 211, 212.

cotton gin machine for separating the fibers of cotton from the seeds, 192.

coun ter at tack (koun'tər ə tak'), *n.* an attack made
in opposition to, or in reprisal for, another
attack, 287.

de fen sive (di fen'siv), *adj.* ready to protect or
defend, 285.

de fraud (di frôd'), *v.t.* take money, rights, etc.,
away from by dishonest means, 236.

de sert (di zėrt'), *v.i.* run away from duty; leave
military service without permission, 291.

div i dend (div'ə dend), *n.* money earned by a company and divided among the owners or stockholders of the company, 231.

dor mi to ry (dôr'mə tôr'ē), *n., pl.* -**ries**. a building with many sleeping rooms, 219.

e con o my (i kon'ə mē), *n., pl.* -**mies**. system of
managing the production, distribution, and
consumption of goods, 230–231.

e man ci pa tion (i man'sə pā'shən), *n.* a release
from slavery, 299.

emi grant (em'ə grənt), *n.* person who leaves his
own country or region to settle in another, 251.

excise tax tax placed on goods made or sold within
a country, 176.

ex pan sion (ek span'shən), *n.* an increasing in size,
256.

148

ex pe di tion (ek'spə dish'ən), *n.* journey for some special purpose, 195.

fa nat ic (fə nat'ik), *n.* person who is carried away beyond reason by his feelings or beliefs, especially in religion or politics, 264.

fron tier (frun tir'), *n.* the farthest part of a settled country. In 1650, the frontier was an imaginary line with white and black settlements on one side and Indian settlements on the other, 197.

fu gi tive (fyü'jə tiv), *n.* person who is fleeing or who has fled from danger, an enemy, justice, etc., 266.

grain drill a horse-drawn instrument which made planting easier, 224.

head wa ters (hed'wô'tərz), *n.* the sources or upper parts of a river, 196.

il lit er ate (i lit'ər it), *adj.* unable to read and write, 303.

immediate cause a cause which has existed for a short time, 183.

im press (im pres'), *v.t.* seize property for public use or force men to serve in the armed forces, 183.

in au gu ra tion (in ô'gyə rā'shən), *n.* act or ceremony of installing a person in office, 181.

in sur rec tion (in 'sə rek'shən), *n.* a rising against established authority; rebellion, 243.

internal improvements in the 1800s, improvements in transportation, which related to turnpikes, steamboats, canals, and railroads, 227.

lib e ra tor (lib'ə rā'tor), *n.* a person who sets others free from slavery, prison, confinement, etc., 299.

manifest destiny the belief that it was God's will that the United States bring progress and democracy to all of North America by increasing its territory, 251.

mar tyr (mär'tər), *n.* person who suffers greatly because of a belief, cause, or principle, 270.

mi nor i ty (mə nôr'ə tē), *n., pl.* -**ties.** group within a country, state, etc., that differs in race, religion, or national origin from the larger part of the population, 235.

mis sion (mish'ən), *n.* headquarters of an organized effort by a religious group to set up churches, schools, hospitals, etc., 254.

mis sion ar y (mish'ə ner'ē), *n., pl.* -**ar ies.** person sent on a religious mission, 251.

mountain men American fur traders who mapped out the best routes over the mountains to the West, 251.

na tion al ism (nash'ə nə liz'əm), *n.* feelings of unity, pride, loyalty, and commitment for one's country, 184, 227, 503.

na tive (nā'tiv), *n.* a person born in a certain place or country, 239.

na tiv ist (nā'tiv ist), *n.* a person who is prejudiced against immigrants, 239.

navigable waterway river or body of water deep enough for ships, 228.

neu tral (nü trəl), *adj.* on neither side in a quarrel or war, 178.

nom i nate (nom'ə nāt), *v.t.,* -**nat ed,** -**nat ing.** name as a candidate for an office, 180.

o ver se er (o'vər sē'ər), *n.* one who oversees others or their work, 222.

pan ic (pan'ik), *n.* an outbreak of widespread alarm, as with people rushing to the banks to get their money out, 233.

par al lel (par'ə lel), *n.* in geography: any of the imaginary circles around the earth parallel to the equator, marking degrees of latitude, 256, 603.

plat form (plat'fôrm), *n.* a statement of a political party's beliefs and a list of the plans it will follow if its members win office, 180.

political party an organization of individuals who have some political interests in common. The goal of a party is to win elections. It provides a platform that candidates agree to follow, nominates candidates for office, and organizes support for candidates, 179.

popular sovereignty a doctrine which meant letting the voters who lived in a territory decide whether or not to allow slavery there, 267.

prej u dice (prej'ə dis), *n.* opinion formed without taking time and care to judge fairly, 235.

pros per i ty (pro sper'ə tē), *n., pl.* -**ties.** profitable business conditions, 233.

Radical Republicans in 1866, Republicans in Congress who thought the South should be punished for starting the Civil War, 306–307.

reap er (rē'pər), *n.* a machine that cuts grain or gathers a crop, 224.

re con struct (rē'kən strukt'), *v.t.* rebuild, 302.

Re con struc tion (rē'kən struk'shən), *n.* a process in which the rebuilding of the Union took place after the Civil War, 302–304.

re cov er y (ri kuv'ər ē), *n., pl.* **-er ies.** a coming back to normal conditions, 233.

re form (ri fôrm'), *v.t.* improve by removing faults, 213.

rotation in office moving officials from one job to another, 212.

scal a wag (skal'ə wag), *n.* a white southerner who joined with the Republicans in the South after the Civil War, 308, 309.

se cede (si sēd'), *v.i.* **-ced ed, -ced ing.** withdraw formally from an organization, 266.

sec tion (sek'shən), *n.* a large area in which people think and work alike. Between 1815 and 1850, the United States had three main sections; the Northeast, the Northwest, and the South, 217.

sec tion al ism (sek shə nə liz'əm), *n.* a feeling of loyalty to a section, 217.

seg re gate (seg'rə gāt), *v.t.,* **-gat ed, -gat ing.** separate or keep apart from others; separate one race of people from another, especially in schools, theaters, etc., 213, 403–404.

share crop ping (sher'krop'ing), *v.t.* farming land for the owner in return for part of the crops, 304.

shuck (shuk), *n.* husk, pod, or shell, especially the outer coverings of corn, chestnuts, etc., 200.

social mobility moving from one social class of people to another, 188.

spark (spärk), *n.* a small bit of fire, 183.

sparse ly (spärs'ly), *adv.* thinly scattered, 194.

spoils system a system in which the people who worked to elect a party's candidates are rewarded with jobs in the government, 212.

squat ter (skwot'ər), *n.* person who settles on public land to acquire ownership of it, 199.

states' rights rights guaranteed to the states by the Constitution, which gives to the states all powers that have not been specifically assigned to the central government or specifically pro-

hibited to the states, 243–244.

strat e gy (strat'ə jē), *n., pl.* **-gies.** the planning and directing of military movements and operations, 285–286.

sub sist ence (səb sis'təns), *n.* means of keeping alive, 227, 230.

suf frage (suf'rij), *n.* the right to vote, 210–211.

sur vey (sər vā'), *v.t.* measure for size, shape, position, boundaries, 223.

tac tic (tak'tik), *n.* a way of acting that is planned to give a certain result, 261.

tem per ance (tem'pər əns), *n.* the principle and practice of not using alcoholic drinks at all, 214–215.

ten e ment (ten'ə mənt), *n.* a building, especially in a poor section of a city, divided into sets of rooms occupied by separate families; a generally run-down building, housing many families, 218, 457.

ter ror ist (ter'ər ist), *n.* person who favors deliberate violence against particular persons or groups, 309.

tra di tion (trə dish'ən), *n.* the handing down of beliefs, opinions, customs, stories, etc. from parents to children, 178.

turn pike (tėrn' pīk') road that has, or used to have, a gate where toll is paid, 227.

u nan i mous (yü nan'ə məs), *adj.* in complete accord or agreement, 175.

underlying cause a cause which is at the basis of a situation, usually existing over a period of time, 183.

va gran cy (vā'grən sē), *n., pl.* **-cies.** a wandering idly from place to place without proper means or ability to earn a living, 306.

var y (ver'ē), *v.t.* **var ied, var y ing.** make different; change, 199.

white supremacy belief that the white race has the highest authority, 309.

zone (zōn), *n.* any region or area especially set off, such as a combat zone where fighting is going on, 297.

Acknowledgments

Illustrations

BA   Bettmann Archive

BB   Brown Brothers

CP   Culver Pictures

LC   Library of Congress

NYHS   The New York Historical Society, New York City

NYPL   The New York Public Library, Astor, Lenox & Tilden Foundations

Cover Based on a photograph by Tom Stack & Associates, Denver.

UNIT 5
172 Linton Park, *Flax Scutching Bee* (detail), National Gallery of Art, Smithsonian Institution **174t** LC **174m** Missouri Historical Society **174b** Anne S. K. Brown Military Collection, Brown University, Providence, R.I. **176** oil by John S. Copley, c. 1763 (detail), Museum of Fine Arts, Boston **177** *Washington Reviewing the Western Army at Fort Cumberland, Maryland*, attributed to James Peale (detail), the Metropolitan Museum of Art, gift of Edgar William and Bernice Chrysler Garbisch, 1963 **181** Historical Society of Pennsylvania **182** Courtesy O.A.S. **184** From *The Pictorial Field-Book of the War of 1812*, p.283, N.Y., 1868 **185** Courtesy, U.S. Naval Academy Museum, Annapolis, Maryland **188** *The Picnic*, anonymous watercolor (detail), the Metropolitan Museum of Art, gift of Edgar William and Bernice Chrysler Garbisch, 1966 **191t** BA **191b** *Pawtucket Bridge & Falls*, Rhode Island Historical Society **195** O. C. Seltzer, *Mountain Man*, the Thomas Gilcrease Institute of American History & Art, Tulsa, Oklahoma **196** From *Trail of Lewis & Clark* by Olin D. Wheeler, 1904 **198** From William A. Crafts: *Pioneers in the Settlement of America*, 1876 Ayer Collection, The Newberry Library, Chicago **199** Details from the Birth & Baptismal Certificate of Margareth Münch, the National Gallery of Art, Washington, Smithsonian Institution, gift of Edgar William and Bernice Chrysler Garbisch **200** LC **201** The Hudson's Bay Company **202** *The Quilting Party* c. 1855, (detail), Abby Aldrich Rockefeller Folk Art Museum **203** Drawing of Flathead Indians by William Clark, 1806, Missouri Historical Society

UNIT 6
206 J.L. Krimmel, *Fourth of July Celebration in Philadelphia*, 1819 (detail), Historical Society of Pennsylvania **208t** Keystone View Co **208m** NYPL, Astor, Lenox & Tilden Foundations **208m** NYHS **208b** NYPL **209** George Caleb Bingham, *Stump Orator*, c. 1850 (detail); Mercantile Library Association, St. Louis. © 1959 by U. of Oklahoma Press, from *George Caleb Bingham: River Portraitist*, by John Francis McDermott **210** CP **212** George Caleb Bingham, *The County Election* (detail); Boatman's National Bank of St. Louis **213** Anonymous, *Girl's Evening School* (detail); Museum of Fine Art, Boston, M. & M. Karolik Collection **214** Sophia Smith Collection, Smith College **215tl & tr** BA **215m** Historical Pictures **218** Scott Foresman Collection **219** LC **222** LC **222** *Harper's Weekly* **224t** *Sewing Grain at Bishops Hill* (detail); Department of Conservation, Bishop Hill,

Illinois **225** watercolor by J. C. Wild, the Cincinnati Historical Society **226** Logbook of Ship William Baker journal kept by George Bliss, 1838. Whaling Museum, New Bedford, Massachusetts **229** Sheet music from The New York State Library **231t** From *Gleason's Pictorial*, October 1854, Scott, Foresman Collection **231b** watercolor by Calyo, Museum of the City of New York **232t** BA **232b** watercolor by Calyo, Museum of the City of New York **236** Courtesy of the American Museum of Natural History, N. Y. **238** Robert Lindneux, *Trail of Tears*, Woolaroc Museum, Bartlesville, Oklahoma **240** Yale University Art Gallery, Mabel Brady Garvan Collection **242l** Cook Collection, Valentine Museum, Richmond, Va. **242r** NYHS **243** William Rubel Collection, photograph courtesy of the National Portrait Gallery, Smithsonian Institution

UNIT 7
248 *Kitchen Ball at White Sulphur Springs*, by Christian Mayr, (detail); Courtesy of the North Carolina Museum of Art, Raleigh **250t** Courtesy of the Texas Memorial Museum, Austin **250m & b** LC **251** BA **253** Denver Public Library, Western History Collection **254** D.R.T. Library at the Alamo **255** BB **258** Lithograph by Sarony & Major, 1848, LC **259** From G. W. Kendall, *The War Between the U.S. & Mexico*, 1851, The Newberry Library, Chicago **263** Charles T. Webber, *The Underground Railway*, (detail); Cincinnati Art Museum **264** BB **265** American Antiquarian Society **270** Historical Pictures, Chicago **271** 1852 lithograph from *Uncle Tom's Cabin*; NYHS **275** LC

UNIT 8
280 From the Collection of Mrs. Nelson A. Rockefeller **282t & m** LC **282b** *Harper's Weekly*, April 4, 1868 **283** oil sketch by Winslow Homer; courtesy, Cooper-Hewitt Museum of Design, Smithsonian Institution **285** LC **286** *N.Y. 7th Regiment*, by Thomas Nast, courtesy, Seventh Regiment Fund, Inc. **287** LC **290l** U. S. Army Photo **290r** LC **291** Detail from *Picket's Charge*, Gettysburg Cyclorama, photograph by Walter Lane **292l & r** LC **293b** LC **295l & r** LC **296** *The Letter Home*, by Eastman Johnson, 1967, M. & M. Karolik Collection; courtesy, Museum of Fine Arts, Boston **297** Photograph by Mathew Brady; courtesy, the American Red Cross **298** LC **299** *Furling the Flag*, by Brooks, West Point Museum Collections, U.S. Military Academy **302** *Frank Leslie's Illustrated Newspaper*, November 30, 1867 **303** Brady Collection, LC **304** *Harper's Weekly*, December 15,

1866 **306** CP **307** BB **308** Nast cartoon from *Harper's Weekly*, November 9, 1872 **309** LC **310l** *Harper's Weekly*, December 19, 1868 **310r** *Harper's Weekly*, July 25, 1868

Quoted Material

Unit 1 **33** John Underhill. Quoted in David Horowitz, THE FIRST FRONTIER. New York: Simon & Schuster, 1978, p. 48. **Unit 2** **67** Municipal Controls—New York City Ordinances: 1731. Cited in URBAN AMERICA: A History With Documents, Bayrd Still. Boston: Little, Brown and Company, 1974, pp. 40-42. **65** Thomas Gray, "Elegy Written in a Country Churchyard," 1750. **58** Mayflower Compact. The Federal and State Constitutions, Colonial Charters, and other Organic Laws of The United States, Part I. Washington: Government Printing Office, 1878. **Unit 3** **88** Joseph Plumb Martin, PRIVATE YANKEE DOODLE. Boston: Little, Brown and Company, 1962, pp. 47-48, 101-102. **90** A Revolutionary Puzzle. Cited in REVOLUTIONARY READER, Sophie Lee Foster, ed. Atlanta, Georgia: Byrd Printing Company, 1913, p. 112. **Unit 7** **251-3** From CONVERSATIONS WITH PIONEER WOMEN by Fred Lockley. Copyright © 1981 by Rainy Day Press. Reprinted by permission. **Unit 5** **201-202** Abridged and adapted from pp. 58-59 (text only) in FRONTIER LIVING by Edwin Tunis (Thomas Y. Crowell Company). Copyright © 1961 by Edwin Tunis. Reprinted by permission of Harper & Row, Publishers, Inc. and Curtis Brown, Ltd. **203** Cited in ORIGINAL JOURNALS OF THE LEWIS AND CLARK EXPEDITION, edited by Reuben Gold Thwaites, Dodd, Mead & Company, 1904-5. **Unit 6** **236** Alexis de Tocqueville, DEMOCRACY IN AMERICA translated from the French, 2 Vols. (London 1835 and 1840). **240** From *Patterns in City Growth* By Joel A. Tarr, © 1975 Scott, Foresman and Company. **Unit 8** **292-294** Civil War letters courtesy Robynn L. Greer. **Unit 10** **375-376** Hamlin Garland, A SON OF THE MIDDLE BORDER. P. F. Collier & Son, 1917. **Unit 11** **396-397** Thomas E. Watson. "The Negro Question in the South." *Arena* (1892), vol. 6, pp. 545-550. **397** Abridged and adapted from pp. 66, 120-122 and 154 in QUEEN OF POPULISTS: THE STORY OF MARY ELIZABETH LEASE by Richard Stiller (Thomas Y. Crowell Company). Copyright © 1970 by Richard Stiller. Reprinted by permission of Harper & Row, Publishers, Inc. **398-399** E. McPherson, ed., *A Handbook of Politics for 1892* (Washington, 1892), pp. 269-271. **406** William Jennings Bryan. *The First Battle: A Story of the Campaign of 1896* (Chicago, 1896), pp. 199-206. **Unit 14** **486** Lithuanian Meat Packer. Anatanas Kaztauskis, "From Lithuania to the Chicago Stockyards," *The Independent*, LVII, 1 (1904), pp. 241 ff. **Unit 15** **527** "Dream Deferred" by Langston Hughes. Copyright 1951 by Langston Hughes. Reprinted from SELECTED POEMS OF LANGSTON HUGHES, by Langston Hughes by permission of Alfred A. Knopf, Inc.

Index

An asterisk (*) after a term means that it is defined in the Glossary.